The Birth of the Babes

Manchester United Youth Policy
1950-57

Tony Whelan

EMPIRE Publications

First published in 2005

EMPIRE PUBLICATIONS
1 Newton Street, Manchester M1 1HW
copyright Tony Whelan 2005

ISBN 1 901 746 45 3

Cover photograph: courtesy of the author
Back cover image of the author courtesy of John Peters, Manchester United FC.
Cover design and layout: Ashley Shaw
Edited by Ashley Shaw and Stuart Fish
Typeset in Caslon and Stone Sans

Printed in Great Britain by Antony Rowe Ltd., Chippenham, Wilts.

CONTENTS

DEDICATION

This book is dedicated to the memory of Jimmy Murphy 1910-1989, without whom!

TONY WHELAN BIOGRAPHICAL DETAILS

TONY WHELAN HAS been deputy assistant Academy Manager at Manchester United Football Club since 1998. A former professional at the club he also played for Manchester City and Rochdale. He spent several years playing in the United States with the Fort Lauderdale Strikers and Atlanta Chiefs in the North American Soccer League (NASL).

On returning to England in 1983 he joined Witton Albion and broke his leg playing for an England non-league representative team at Altrincham FC in March 1984. Following this he spent many years working as an education social worker prior to joining the academy staff full-time.

A fully qualified FA Coach, Tony also has a BA in Humanities from the Open University and a MA in Sociology from Manchester Metropolitan University. He is married to Patricia and has two children Marc and Nadine.

ACKNOWLEDGEMENTS

THIS BOOK WAS originally an MA thesis submitted to the Manchester Metropolitan University in 1999 for a degree in Sociology. Having seen it sitting on library bookshelves I was encouraged by friends and colleagues who read it to seek to get it published so that it could be read by a wider audience. They felt that former players as well as fans would be interested in the subject matter.

To this end I approached Stuart Fish and Ashley Shaw at Empire Publications who without hesitation saw it as a worthwhile project and undertook the task of transferring an academic tome into a book suitable for popular readership. I am indebted to them for their hard work and dedication in bringing it to fruition.

The completion of a book of this nature necessarily involves the support of many people. I wish to express my gratitude to Sir Alex Ferguson for not only reading the original thesis but kindly writing the Foreword despite his various commitments. I am also indebted to Terry Beckett, Laurie Cassidy, Bill Foulkes, Frank Hannah and Albert Scanlon for giving up their time to be interviewed for the project. I thank them for their kindness and considerable patience. I am especially grateful to Joe Armstrong and Wilf McGuinness for not only agreeing to be interviewed but for providing photographs and other memorabilia.

I am also indebted to the staff at the Manchester United Museum, particularly Mark Wylie, the Curator, and his former assistant Zoe Makinson, for putting up with my various requests to examine the archives. My thanks also, to Cliff Butler at Manchester United for writing the introduction as well as providing me with important statistical information and John Peters for his kind permission in allowing me to reproduce a few of his photographs. Thanks are also due to Nick Murphy for his kindness and generosity in loaning his personal copy of his father's memoirs, and to Paul McGuinness for giving me time and space when I needed it. The Professional Footballers' Association have supported my studies over a number of years, I am extremely grateful to them.

I am also indebted to Phil Vasili who does not realise what a font of support and encouragement he has been to me. I am also grateful to my sister, Maria, for making time in her busy schedule to type my manuscripts.

Considerable gratitude is due to Dr Ken Parsons at Manchester Metropolitan University for his advice, guidance and assistance. It would be remiss if I failed to acknowledge the encouragement I have received from everyone at the Manchester United Academy. We are the proud and privileged guardians of a wonderful legacy which was established all those years ago. The torch that was ignited then, continues to burn brightly.

Finally, heartfelt thanks are due to Patricia, my wife and my children Marc and Nadine. Without their love and support this book would never have been completed.

Tony Whelan

February 2005

FOREWORD

THERE ARE FEW events football supporters enjoy more than seeing a young player, who has made his way through the club's junior, youth and reserve teams, make his debut in the senior side.

Don't get me wrong, I know they also take great delight in seeing the arrival of a big-money signing, but they've always attached an extra-special significance to the introduction of a youngster who's been at the club since schooldays, into the senior side.

Manchester United fans have always been unswerving in their support of homegrown talent particularly since the 1950s and the days of the 'Busby Babes'.

Even as a young man growing up in Glasgow I was aware of the impact young players were having on United's fortunes.

Their exploits in the FA Youth Cup, during the first five seasons of the competition, were widely publicised bringing names like Duncan Edwards, Eddie Colman, Liam Whelan, Wilf McGuinness and Bobby Charlton to everyone's attention.

All those players, many many more, were to become great names in the club's history alongside the men who charted their astronomical progress through the ranks: Matt Busby, Jimmy Murphy and the backroom staff of the day.

'If they're good enough, they're old enough' was Busby and Murphy's philosophy and introducing young players *en bloc* to the first team was to prove a masterstroke and paid great dividends in the mid-1950s as United developed into one of the best club sides in Europe.

Only the terrible tragedy at Munich airport in February 1958, which claimed the lives of eight players and three staff amongst a total of 23 fatalities, prevented them from stamping an even more indelible mark on the game.

The working practices, coaching systems and overall provision for young players, which were set in place all of those years ago, are still prevalent to this day.

Our current training complex at Carrington, in south-west Manchester, is amongst the best of its type anywhere, but structures, facilities and state-of-the-art equipment are only part of the overall package.

That's all backed up by educational, welfare and medical departments which are geared to give the young players the best possible start to adult life and the opportunity to make a career in professional football.

It may not have been quite so sophisticated back in the 1950s but even then it was much more than just taking boys on the books straight from school and instantly turning them into famous footballers.

We all owe a huge debt of gratitude to Tony Whelan for bringing to us the full fascinating story behind Manchester United's hugely successful youth policy of the 1950s.

His research on this project has been thorough and it is plainly obvious that there wasn't an avenue he didn't explore in search of information, first hand accounts and interviews with people involved at the time.

Tony Whelan, a respected and prized member of the current Academy coaching staff at Carrington, has proved, with publication of the fine book, that he's certainly got more than one string to his bow.

Sir Alex Ferguson
Manager
Ferburary 2005

PREFACE

MANCHESTER UNITED is justifiably proud of its reputation for discovering, developing and nurturing young footballers. For well over half a century they have been at the forefront of producing some of British Isles' most talented young players.

Hundreds of eager youngsters have taken their place on the famed Old Trafford conveyor belt in that time and whilst there are many who failed to make the whole journey, those who did, and continue to do so, have been rewarded with fame and, in later years at least, fortune.

The history of Manchester United and its forerunners Newton Heath has been lovingly documented by numerous historians and statisticians over the years but it is only recently that the various eras of the club have been singled out for more detailed analysis.

This latest addition to the already extensive Manchester United compendium of literature tells the story, in meticulously researched detail, of the early days of United's 'academy'.

Academy is the modern description for the section of professional clubs that deals with the production of young players, but it is a title that wouldn't have been out of place back in the middle decades of the last century.

The foundations of United's youth development system were laid down before the Second World War when the Manchester United Junior Athletic Club (MUJAC) was set up. But it wasn't until Matt Busby and Jimmy Murphy teamed up following the cessation of hostilities that the club's youth policy really took off.

Busby and Murphy set about transforming Manchester United from being an underachieving big-city club into one of the most famous sporting institutions to be found anywhere in the world.

United had shuttled back and forth between the top two divisions in the inter-war years but it didn't take long for the two great men to bring stability to the ailing giant. And, it wasn't long before success followed in the shape of the FA Cup in 1948 and, four years later, the League championship.

Busby and Murphy weren't, however, prepared to rest on their laurels and in the midst of their early successes they were quietly preparing for the future.

They were putting into place the mechanism that was to produce a stream of young players who would eventually take over from the old guard and ultimately carve for themselves a unique place in Manchester United history.

That group of young starlets was to become known as the 'Busby Babes' as they helped to forge a burgeoning reputation for the club at home and overseas.

Five solid years of success in the FA Youth Cup helped the club to attain a growing reputation in the sphere of nurturing young talent. It's a label the club retains to this very day.

They also extended their routes of success across the continent, most famously in the prestigious Blue Star Youth Tournament in Zurich, Switzerland.

The full story behind this defining era of the club had never really been covered in any depth until Tony Whelan set about the task as part of a degree course in 1999.

No stone was left unturned as he sought to reveal the fascinating background to the club's youth policy of the 1950s.

The legacy of those now far-off days is still enjoyed in the early years of the third Millennium as the club's extensive scouting network, coaching system and back-up staff continues to produce players of world-class calibre.

United's fame now stretches to every country and territory on earth. It's a global recognition that really began to take shape post-Second World War.

Accordingly, this excellent account of those days also uncovers, in some detail, the embryonic moments of Manchester United's incredible universal fame and attraction.

Cliff Butler
Manchester United Statistician
February 2005

INTRODUCTION

MANCHESTER UNITED have long been renowned for producing their own players through an active and vibrant youth policy. This tradition continues today. Indeed, the club achieved an unprecedented 'treble' in 1999 by winning the European Cup, Premier League, and the FA Cup in the same season with a squad of players, several of whom had been developed via the youth policy: David Beckham, Wes Brown, Nicky Butt, Ryan Giggs, Phil and Gary Neville and Paul Scholes.

The origin of Manchester United's youth policy goes back more than sixty years, but the primary aim of this study is to focus on a very specific period of United's youth policy - 1950-1957 - to analyse the reasons why the club were so successful in producing their own players during this particular period. During this time they gave several teenagers their first team debuts and won the FA Youth Cup for five consecutive years 1953-54-55-56-57.

MANCHESTER UNITED HAVE ALWAYS RELIED HEAVILY ON THEIR YOUTH RESOURCES. THE TWO EUROPEAN CUP WINNING TEAMS ARE A CASE IN POINT - IN 1968 EIGHT MEMBERS OF THE WINNING TEAM CAME FROM THE YOUTH RANKS, OF THE TREBLE WINNING SQUAD OF 1999, SEVEN EMERGED FROM THE SAME SYSTEM.

It is hoped that this study will provide a clearer understanding of the particular social context in which the youth policy at Manchester United was created and implemented. That is, the general state of football in post-war Britain and the attempt by Manchester United to address what they perceived to be a particular problem. This was the singular lack of good young players graduating through the existing youth programme who were capable of playing in the first team.

However, exactly what do we mean when we talk about a youth policy? In the context of this study the term youth policy refers to Manchester United's systematic selection, recruitment, coaching and training of young footballers between the age of fifteen and eighteen with the express aim of establishing them in the first team. It also refers to Matt Busby's philosophy of football - his belief that young players should be taught to play in a certain way; that they should be allowed to express themselves as individuals on the field. United were not the only club who sought to develop a youth policy in the immediate post-war period. As we shall examine, albeit briefly, the youth policy at Wolverhampton Wanderers was very highly regarded - the Midlanders were seen by many as United's main rivals in the development of youth in this period.

The research will also seek to explain the extent to which the club's ethos - the emphasis on youth - was a reflection of Busby's wider political and social beliefs (his socialism) germinating from his upbringing in a Lanarkshire mining village, Bellshill, in which family, kin, and community were so important.

There exists a considerable amount of literature on a range of topics relating to football as Peter Seddon's *A Football Compendium: A Complete Guide to the Literature in Football* demonstrates. However, there has been very little research into the development of youth players at professional football clubs. This book will look at some of the literature in the field: the social history of football, sociology, and theory. This will help to place the study within a sound conceptual framework.

There are an abundance of books about Manchester United in the form of general histories, biographies, and autobiographies of players, as well as statistical information. We will see that many of these books touch on aspects of United's youth policy but only in a general way. This seems a strange omission given that the youth policy at the club has been held in such high esteem over the years. This is especially true with regard to the pre-Munich team affectionately known as 'The Busby Babes' whose exploits at junior level have generally gone unnoticed.

Consequently, there has been little research on the youth policy at Manchester United during the fifties that could be called coherent and systematic. This book attempts to map out unexplored territory which other researchers could take further.

It is felt that the research is worthwhile because of the need to explain how the club was able to produce so many outstanding players during the fifties through their youth system. These players included Bobby Charlton and Duncan Edwards, considered by many to be two of the finest players ever to grace the game in this country. I have argued that such players did not arrive on the scene suddenly, abruptly - but rather they were the fruits of a dynamic process of youth development at the club about which little is generally known. My aim is to contribute to a greater understanding of the processes by which the club undertook its hugely successful youth policy in the fifties.

The research also has value for me for another reason: as a product of the club's youth programme in the late sixties and early seventies, I signed for the club as an apprentice professional in July 1968 shortly after they had become the first English team to win the European Cup. Matt Busby (whose philosophy of football dominates this study) was still the Manager. The principles and values I was taught at the club had a lineage that began many years before, beginning with Busby's arrival as Manager in 1945. These values had an impact on me and I still try to impart them to the young players at Manchester United today as a Coach in the Football Academy.

The Football Academy at Manchester United takes boys between the ages of nine and sixteen and they receive coaching during the evening and play for the club's junior teams on a Sunday morning. There is a marked difference between this programme and the one that prevailed in the fifties.

I became interested in the history of the club's youth policy after listening to stories by other coaches like Nobby Stiles (a former player and World Cup Winner 1966) discussing the club's coaching and training methods when he first joined the club in the late fifties. I found this information fascinating and developed an urge to find out more. Alas, very little of this information is actually recorded because like so much of football history, it is only transmitted orally. However, as Rogan Taylor and Andrew Ward have said regarding the value of an oral approach to football research,

"Football research calls out for a genre that is loyal to the sport's emotional truth. Spoken history is how football preserves its own stories. Spoken history is what the sport deserves."

Having been a professional footballer for sixteen years I can vouch for the veracity of this statement. Most professional footballers do not write their autobiographies or memoirs, so the oral history method gives them a voice that otherwise would not be heard. In this sense it is much more democratic because it is not just the opinions of the more famous names that are being heard, but rather people from every strata of the game: players, spectators, referees, managers, coaches and administrators. Oral history lends itself to football research because it is by its very nature creative and co-operative in its methodology. It is also extremely flexible because it can collect evidence precisely where it is needed. This is especially true in the case of this study. For example, in an interview with former Manchester United player Wilf McGuinness I was able to acquire valuable oral testimony relating to the youth team's first tour to Switzerland in 1954.

Another former player, Albert Scanlon, gave me an insight into working conditions on the club's groundstaff in the early fifties. Oral history is also personal, it is about individual lives and experiences and any life is of interest especially if that life can throw light on specific areas of human interest that would not be possible by any other means. The tape recorder allows history to be recorded orally, but also 'presented' through the spoken word. This does not mean that the oral historian does not refer to other sources - on the contrary, oral history is a means of interpreting the past as an alternative and complement to the documents normally used by historians.

In fact oral history has a tradition that goes back as far as ancient Greece where descriptions of armour, name and lists of abandoned cities were preserved orally for 600 years before being written down in the *Iliad*, the Great Poem of antiquity. Many of these descriptions have been verified by classical scholars.

The leading French historian of the 19th Century, Jules Michelet, when writing his *History of the French Revolution* assumed that written documents constituted but one source among many others. His primary aim in using oral evidence was to 'counterbalance' the official documents with the 'judgements of popular tradition'. The oral history method is used today by many scholars especially sociologists and anthropologists, who would not consider themselves to be historians. This is because documentary evidence is not always reliable, newspaper bias is an obvious example. Furthermore, oral evidence can and often does contradict documentary sources. Many conventional sources that social historians use, for example the census, registrations of birth, marriage, death and social surveys are themselves based on interviews.

Accordingly, I believe that the oral history approach outlined above is the best method of analysing Manchester United's Youth Policy in the fifties. This method was correlated with other documentary evidence culled from the club's archives. This included minutes of Board meetings, details of contracts, examination of player passes, programmes, artefacts, and general memorabilia.

During the course of this project I was granted virtually unrestricted access to information germane to this study. I was also granted privileged access to the personal papers and records of former players of the club which would not have been possible using non-oral methodology. For example during an interview at his home, Wilf McGuinness allowed me to peruse his extensive private collection of football memorabilia gathered during his playing days. This contained various kinds of documentary evidence relevant to this study including letters, newspaper articles, photographs, programmes and so on.

In the sphere of football research the value of oral evidence is clear. Although there exists a wealth of documentary evidence relating to Manchester United, much that I wished to find out regarding the club's youth policy was either treated sketchily or not touched on at all. Therefore, I found that many of the questions the research was seeking to answer, in relation to Manchester United's youth policy in the fifties, could only be answered via oral testimony. Thus an anecdotal approach was the best method of gathering the evidence required in order to get a more complete understanding of the period in question.

But to what extent can oral evidence be considered reliable? In the case of this study, some oral testimony can be corroborated by documentary sources - but in other cases this has not been possible because no such evidence exists. Thus this evidence must be taken on its own merit. However, this is also true of other sources as we have seen.

With regard to this study, all the people interviewed were valuable eye-witnesses of the events they describe. In my opinion they had absolutely no reason to be less than forthright with their responses because the nature of the questions asked were in no way

controversial or contentious (see appendix).

It would be appropriate at this point to introduce the interviewees whose evidence is a thread which runs throughout this book. They have been chosen because they are especially qualified to comment on the events they describe.

JOE ARMSTRONG JUNIOR is the son of Joe Armstrong who was the Chief Scout at Manchester United during the fifties. He was a player himself, having the distinction of playing for the United 'Colts', a junior team, in 1943. Joe has been a part-time scout at Manchester United for many years and has managed the junior teams from time-to-time when requested. His testimony is important because he has vivid memories of his father's scouting methods during the period of this study. He also had a wealth of documentary evidence such as his father's diaries and personal papers which the author was privileged to peruse.

LAURIE CASSIDY was a former player at Manchester United whom he joined in 1947. He played in the first team, but most of his football at the club was played in the reserves where he was valued as a mentor of the junior players. Laurie left the club n 1956 and had a spell with Oldham Athletic before retiring in 1957. He then qualified as a teacher and became involved with the Manchester Schools Football Association (MSFA). He was the team manager of the Manchester Boys under-fifteen team for several years. Now in retirement, Laurie remains a life member of the MSFA. Laurie's testimony provides an insight into the relationship between the Manchester Schools FA and Manchester United in the fifties. He also had some rare copies of MSFA handbooks published in the period containing extremely valuable material pertaining to this study - the author would never have discovered this important evidence by any other means.

FRANK HANNAH has been President of the Manchester County FA since 1975. He became a member of the FA Council in 1979 and a Vice-President of the Football Association (a considerable honour) in 1998. Frank is a qualified referee and he officiated in many games involving Manchester United's junior teams during the fifties. He sheds some light on the playing conditions Manchester United's junior players encountered during the period.

TERRY BECKETT played for Manchester Boys for two years as well as Lancashire and England schoolboys in 1953 and 1954. He signed amateur forms for Manchester United in 1954 and became a professional in 1956. Terry played in the FA Youth Cup final for

United in 1955 when they defeated West Bromwich Albion. Terry is still involved at the club as he has been a part-time scout since 1984. His testimony is important because as a former Manchester Schools player he is well acquainted with Manchester United's scouting methods during the fifties. He also travelled to Zurich, Switzerland on tour. His recollections of these experiences make a valuable contribution to a more complete understanding of United's involvement in youth competitions in the fifties.

BILL FOULKES is a Manchester United legend. He joined the club in 1950 and went on to make 679 appearances for the first team before retiring in 1970. Bill won four League championship medals and one FA Cup winners' medal in 1963. His crowning achievement was winning a European Cup winners' medal in 1968 at the age of 36. Bill was a survivor of the 1958 Munich air disaster in which many of his team-mates and friends were killed. It says much for his character and spirit that he recovered so well from this tragic event, and went on to have an extremely distinguished career. Bill was at the club throughout the period of this study. Therefore, his evidence regarding the coaching and training methods used is invaluable.

ALBERT SCANLON was also a Munich survivor, a former Manchester Schoolboy star he joined United as an amateur in 1950 and became a full professional in 1952. Albert played 127 matches for the first team, scoring 35 goals. He also played in the last match the pre-Munich side played, in Yugoslavia against Red Star Belgrade. Whilst a junior at the club, Albert won two FA Youth Cup winners' medals in 1953 and 1954 and went on the youth team tour to Switzerland in 1954. This was the first time the club had ventured abroad with a youth team.

Albert was able to give detailed descriptions of what it was like to work at the club as a member of the groundstaff in the fifties. He also provides a fascinating glimpse of what it was like to play in the club's junior teams during this period. Albert told me that he has no memorabilia from his playing days, as it was given away by his father over the years. This makes his oral evidence even more significant because, as he says himself, "all I have left are my memories".

WILF McGUINNESS had the distinction of captaining Manchester, Lancashire and England schoolboys and he joined Manchester United in 1953 on leaving school. He signed professional forms in November 1954. Wilf went on to make 85 first team appearances before a broken leg in December 1959 ended his career. He was then appointed youth

ALBERT SCANLON WEARING HIS BELOVED UNITED BLAZER. ALBERT WAS PRIVVY TO THE DAY-TO-DAY WORKING OF THE FOOTBALL CLUB IN HIS ROLE AS A GROUNDSTAFFER.

team coach at the club which he combined with the post of England youth team trainer between 1963 and 1969. Wilf was also appointed to the England coaching staff by Alf Ramsey for the 1966 World Cup. He was appointed United's first team coach in June 1969 and then Manager in 1970 before leaving the club to manage in Greece. Wilf played in three successive Youth Cup winning sides for United between 1954 and 1956 and, like Albert Scanlon, he went on the youth team's first trip to Switzerland in 1954. Wilf has spoken eloquently about the coaching at the club during the fifties and he gives splendid accounts of Manchester United's exploits in youth cup competitions. He also gave me access to his private papers which were extremely rich and varied and provided the author with a wealth of valuable material for this study. It was an extremely humbling experience for me to handle this material and to inform Wilf that he did not realise the significance of his collection.

It goes without saying that it is not possible to interview all the candidates who could have contributed to this research. The above people are therefore a representative group and this should be kept in mind whilst reading this book.

WILF McGUINNESS: SERVED UNITED AS A PLAYER, COACH AND MANAGER DURING A 20-YEAR SPELL AT THE CLUB.

CHAPTER ONE: HISTORY AND SOCIOLOGY

This chapter attempts to examine some general sociological theories which have been used to explain the phenomenon we call sport. It will go on to look at three theories which are specific to football in general and this research in particular. In order to elucidate the role of theory, this chapter will include an analysis and review of what has been written about the social history of football in general and Manchester United in particular. Finally, it will go on to deal more specifically with Manchester United's youth policy tracing its pre-war origins to the revolutionary development by Matt Busby in the late 1940s. Concentration will be primarily on Manchester United, but the youth policy at Wolverhampton Wanderers will be discussed as a comparative model of a rival club.

ORBERT ELIAS, THE renowned sociologist, recounts a discussion with his colleague Eric Dunning regarding the academic credibility and respectability of studying sport, especially football, for an MA dissertation. He was concerned that the authorities at Leicester University where he taught would not see football as a legitimate sphere for post-graduate work. He went to great lengths to define the academic integrity of football research and it is to his enormous credit that Leicester University now has a thriving MSc programme in the sociology of sport that attracts students from all over the world.

An attempt has been made to confer 'respectability' and 'ancestry' to the sociology of sport by pointing to oblique references in the work of classical sociologists like Weber. However, the sociology of sport is a relatively recent area of academic interest, and its growth has been quite substantial since the 1960s especially in the United States, Canada and Germany. Its existence has historically been within the field of physical education where work is primarily of a practical nature. Physical Educationalists have tended to write about problems specific to physical culture and sport, but have generally omitted to draw out social connections.

Until recently work in the sociology of sport has generated little interest within mainstream sociology, football hooliganism being a notable exception, attracting the attention of Marxist and deviancy sociologists. This is exemplified by the MA thesis submitted by Anthony Giddens (London School of Economics) in 1961 in an area of the sociology of sport. He has since earned his academic reputation as a sociological theorist of the first order in all areas of the discipline.

The reason that sport has been neglected in sociology according to Elias is that "sport was not - or, perhaps more properly, it was not - perceived by the 'founding fathers' to be the locus of serious social problems at the time when the basic contours of modern sociology were being formed". This led to the neglect of the sociology of sport in academic inquiry. Furthermore, sociology has tended to be restricted to the 'serious', or 'rational' sphere of human experience with the result that human urges for 'fun', 'play' and 'pleasurable excitement' have received limited attention in sociological theory and research. Despite this, there can be absolutely no doubt about the social significance of sport which attracts great interest. Important areas of sporting interest include: sport as leisure, sport as work, employment patterns and social mobility in sport, amateur and professionalism, race, gender and violence.

The importance of the Football World Cup and Olympic Games make them ripe for sociological research as is the impact of boycotting sports events as weapons in international relations. Indeed Lawrence Kitchin has suggested that soccer is "the only global idiom apart from science" (Elias and Dunning 1986). Elias further concludes that studying sport without studying society are "studies out of context".

Having established the social context of sport we shall now examine various theories of sport which sociologists in the field have formulated in order to reach a better understanding of the role of sport in society. Dunning has argued that theory in sport is not very well advanced and he related the formulation of grand theories on sport to scientific methodology. Dunning offers the following definition of the role of theory in the sociology of sport:

> *"Theories serve in the analysis and interpretation of known facts... they also serve as guides to future research by helping one to formulate questions and by suggesting in the form of hypotheses trends and relationships which seem probable."*

In this manner theories may help to direct research into "systematically related channels". The author has found this definition extremely helpful as a means of focusing on the theories relevant to this study.

Until the 1970s two general theories of social life informed questions about the relationship between sport and society: functionalist and conflict theory. Both theories are based on different assumptions about the foundations of social order which lead to different questions about social life and the role of sport within it. These obviously lead to different conclusions.

Functionalist theorists believe that the primary motivation underlying social life is the tendency for any social system to maintain itself in a state of balance or equilibrium. In order to operate efficiently social systems naturally seek a balance through an emphasis on common values, consensus and co-operation. When this balance is upset society becomes dysfunctional. Sociologists using functionalist theory have tended to ask questions about how sports fit into social life contributing to stability and social progress within communities. This has led to questions about the ways that sports contribute to 'basic needs' of social systems. In summary, functionalist theory focuses attention on how sports satisfy the fundamental needs of society. The other general theory used to explain the role of sport in society is Marxism or conflict theory. Marx did not write specifically about sport, but his theories can certainly be applied to it. The crux of Marx's work was an analysis of modern capitalism, an economic system based on a distinction between the owners of the means of production (factories, land, equipment) - the bosses whose interest capitalism serves. On the other hand, the working class (proletariat) have only their labour power to sell. Because the system does not work for them, they must be persuaded that it could, if only they would work harder or had more good fortune. The bosses maxim is: 'there is nothing wrong with the system, rather it is the workers who need to change their attitude'. Once they are convinced that it is actually working 'for' them capitalism is not challenged or placed under threat. In other words, capitalism has developed a methodology to ensure its own survival - this is precisely where sport has a role to play.

Meanwhile, Hargreaves (Cashmore 1990) argues that sports help to keep the population pacified or docile. He juxtaposes sport and industry and makes comparisons between them for example: specialisation, standardisation, bureaucracy, productivity, hierarchical administration, and so on. This ultimately produces alienation of both producer and consumer, epitomised by global events such as the World Cup and Olympic Games. Thus sports become an opiate of the people, akin to the Roman *Panem et Circensus* (Bread and Circuses) used by the nobles to placate the *plebs* (Mob). In the end, the sports performer is commercialised, becoming a commodity used by capitalists: produced, packaged and sold like any other commodity. This is referred to as 'commodification'.

Critical theorists say that sports work in subtle ways, attributing values to people which are mirrored in society as a whole. These are capitalist values such as individualism, competitiveness and so on. They are seen as admirable qualities within a sporting context and are unquestioned.

Jean Marie-Brohm (Cashmore 1990) has argued vigorously that sport is in no sense an alternative to work nor an escape from it since it removes physical freedom and spontaneity. The competitor is a mere prisoner whose performance is recorded, evaluated and controlled. In this way capitalism restricts human imagination as the body becomes a mere machine: "obeying the logic of the system". This strikes against notions of individualism, self-expression and improvisation which are crucial in understanding Matt Busby's philosophy / sociology of football which inform many of the questions I am seeking to answer.

Functionalist and conflict theories are not the only ones that have been used in order to explain the influence of sport in society. It would be remiss of me if I failed to mention the influential work of Norbert Elias , who expounded the theory of the *Civilising Process* in his *magnum opus* (1994). This is an extremely complex and erudite work and what follows is a mere outline of the theory.

Elias uses the term 'civilising process' to describe a movement, trend or evolution within human societies that seeks to control the level of violence and to encourage the observance of manners. He attempts to show that the social norms of conduct and customs among the upper classes began to change quite rapidly from the 16th Century onwards in a specific way. The social rules of conduct gradually became more fixed, differentiated and all-embracing with an emphasis on temperance and pacification. Violence and aggression were becoming less acceptable methods of settling conflicts and disputes.[1] This development was expressed in a term used by the humanist scholar Erasmus to describe a new refinement in manners encapsulated in the term 'civility'. Civilised societies create their own tension and devise counter-measures against such tensions which conform to comparative sensitivities to physical violence. The resolution of problems and disputes by means other than violence is central to Elias's theory and he uses the development of the Parliamentary system in England after the Civil War as an example. Guttmann (1986) has also dealt with the issue of violence in sport but from the standpoint of the spectators through the ages.

We shall now go on to look at other theories which have specific relevance to this research. The first two are within the sphere of sociology, the third falls within the field of Educational Theory.

Elias and Dunning have looked at "the dynamics of sports with particular reference to football". They are not concerned with issues connected directly to the sociology of sport but rather they attempt to clarify the sociological concept of 'configuration'. They use the analysis of football as a means to develop a critique of small group research in sociology as well as addressing the failure of sociological theorists to produce a unified theory which can account for the nature of conflict in human relations.

Small group research has generally been concerned to conduct experiments in group behaviour under strictly controlled laboratory conditions. This is to conform with scientific methodology. Elias and Dunning see this as a mistake because, "it is impossible to simulate 'real life' social structures and social situations in the laboratory". Evidence is highly formulised and artificial, doing little to aid understanding of behaviour and social structures in society as a whole. Therefore, groups such as football teams have more relevance, it is argued, as subjects for sociological research. It is crucial that they are studied as 'social configurations'. Elias and Dunning argue that what takes place on the football field, that is, the interaction within and between the opposing team, can only be completely understood by focusing on the interdependence of the teams as a part of a 'single configuration". They assert that football is a 'game' which involves the changing configurations of players as they move about the field interchanging positions in relation to the movement of the ball and other players. One can observe the players moving around the field in constant interdependence forming ever changing configurations. However, the physical context does not change i.e. the goal posts and pitch markings remain constant.[2] This can be applied to society in general though the actual configurations are more difficult to observe i.e. cities, church goers, political parties and so on.

Sports games like football can be a useful introduction to a configurational approach to the study of tension and conflict. The focus is not on one side or the other, but between the dynamics of both together - a single 'Configuration in tension'. A central characteristic in football is the manner in which tension in groups is kept under control or harnessed. This was not so in the past, see *Folk football in medieval and early modern Britain* in Dunning (Ed) (1971) where it is argued that violence has diminished over time and organisation (for example since the founding of the Football Association in 1863) has led to self restraint or civilising. One is reminded of Elias's theory!

Elias and Dunning's work is extremely useful as a means of looking at Manchester

United in the early 1950s as a single social group or configuration with its own tensions and tension controls. This book seeks to explore and explain the various dynamics which were operating at the club at various levels: issues of status, rivalry and competition. How was this tension controlled? Elias and Dunning believe that studies of sports like football may help in understanding issues of tension and conflict within society as a whole. Issues such as class, race, competition and so forth. All these are germane to the questions the author is seeking to answer in relation to Manchester United's youth programme in the 1950s.[3]

Another theory that impinges on Matt Busby's philosophy of football is the thesis advanced by Johan Huizinga in *Homo Ludens* (Man the player 1970). Huizinga argues that play is behaviour which involves freedom from constraints. Freedom is essential for innovation and the development of culture. For Huizinga, play is defined in the broad sense in that it includes the creative work of scientists, artists, musicians, writers and so on. He argues that man's ability to play has formed the basis of all culture and civilisation. Man has always played, and it could be argued that all discoveries and inventions have been a by-product of play. Thus play is the foundation-stone of sport because all sport has its origins in play.

Huizinga argues that in the 19th century, due to increasing industrialisation, the 'natural' play element was lost. Industrialisation made life more regimented and stifled innovation. In this sense modern sports with their rules and bureaucracy do not represent true forms of play. He states that: "in the case of sport we have an activity nominally known as play but raised to such a pitch of technical organisation and scientific thoroughness that the real play-spirit is threatened with extinction". This applies especially to professional sports people for whom, "the true play-spirit is lacking". Huizinga's theory has been helpful in that it could be applied to Matt Busby's concept / philosophy of 'getting back' to the more natural play forms that existed during his own football development. That is the belief that players must be allowed to experiment and explore the limits of their talent without undue regimentation or constraints. This would lead to the full blossoming of potential as well as leading to more artistic and creative play. One immediately thinks of George Best as being the example *par excellence* of this philosophy.

The final theory I will consider is that of the role of aesthetics in sport with particular reference to football. Studies in this sphere have generally come under the jurisdiction of education and not sociological theory. However, aesthetics is an area that has a major bearing on this study in the light of Matt Busby's idea of football being 'a beautiful game' ie that it has aesthetic qualities.[4]

An important concept in the field of aesthetics is that of 'mastery'. In education the concept of mastery implies that something can actually be taught, be it a physical movement or a particular methodology. In football this could be a technical or tactical movement. Since mastery can be taught by a teacher it must conform to rules or theoretical concepts which are generally accepted. In an essay *Sport and Art - the concept of mastery* in Whiting and Masterson (1974) Hans Keller argued that there are great talents in sport who are not allowed to develop because they are being harmed rather than helped by practice. The rules of mastery only tell a performer what is not new, that is, what can be taught in a formal way. It does not write prescriptions for things that are not new. Therefore, mastery is 'playing by the rules'. However, it is the creative genius who continues to improvise thus formulating 'new' rules but then making these new rules obsolete.

One only has to look at the great performers in most sports to see just how true this is: Muhammad Ali, Garry Sobers and Pelé are excellent examples.[5] This book seeks to examine the role of Matt Busby and his coaching staff as teachers or educators (Chapter Four). How far did Matt Busby's philosophy of football conform to the prevailing ideas about the way football was played: technically, tactically and aesthetically?

THE HISTORY OF FOOTBALL

History and sociology are bedfellows - they are complementary rather than antagonistic towards each other. We will now review what has been written about the social history of football in general and Manchester United in particular in order to place this study within a sound contextual framework. It will go on to trace the origins of Manchester United's youth policy and its development by Matt Busby. Much research in the history of football has been centred on 'major' events such as the FA, European and World Cups. Great players have also received considerable attention.[6] However, there has been very little research into youth development at football clubs. (see Introduction)

Young (1968), Walvin (1975), Mason (1980) and Fishwick (1989) have produced excellent studies on the major social aspects of football dealing with a range of issues from the rise of the clubs in England to overseas influences. Fishwick's book is of particular interest because it was originally a DPhil thesis (Oxford 1984), and it takes up the history of football from where Mason ends (1915) to the beginning of this study (1950). Both writers deal with the recruitment and development of youth at football clubs but only fleetingly. Mason examines in some detail the origins of tactical development in football during its early years.

Green (1974) is of special interest because he focuses on soccer in the 1950s. He discusses in detail the major events and personalities of the decade as well as tactical developments in England and Europe. Green believes that this decade was the most important of the century because of all the events which took place. Events such as the 'Matthews' Cup Final (1953) and Manchester United's entry into the European Cup in 1956, the first English team to enter the competition.

Taylor and Ward (1995) have looked at football history from the standpoint of the very people who were involved or witnessed it: players, managers, officials, spectators and administrators. It is the only 'oral' history of football published to date containing information that could only have been exclusively gleaned from oral sources. The book is important because it contains an excellent chapter on coaching and training during the 1950s that applies to this area of research. However, Taylor and Ward have nothing to say specifically about youth football.

Hopcraft (1968) has also explored the nature of football through the eyes of the players, managers and directors. It is written by a distinguished football correspondent who

BILLY WRIGHT AND FERENC PUSKAS LEAD ENGLAND AND
HUNGARY OUT AT WEMBLEY IN 1953. IT WOULD PROVE TO BE ONE OF THE
MOST SIGNIFICANT MATCHES IN ENGLISH FOOTBALL HISTORY.

offers an unusual insight to the game from the 'inside' as it were.[7] The book contains a brief sketch of Matt Busby's management, including his youth policy. Hugo Meisl's (1955) study encapsulates the continuing debate during our period about the perceived decline in playing standards in England. He argues that English football has been in decline since 1926 when the offside law was changed. This resulted in a 'safety first' attitude amongst football managers and coaches with a concentration on the physical aspects of the game as opposed to artistry and skill. This was exposed comprehensively in 1953 when the Hungarians defeated England 6 - 3 at Wembley. This was their first-ever defeat on home soil by foreign opposition and shocked the football world. Meisl asserts unequivocally that the aesthetic aspects of the game were being neglected to the detriment of English football. Meisl's book offers an understanding of the technical and tactical football climate in England in which Busby worked. It also demonstrates that there were voices in the game (Busby's included) who believed that artistry and self-expression were essential features of the game and they wanted to see change. The quest for a return to the aesthetics of the game was an important aspect of Busby's philosophy of football.

There are an abundance of books about Manchester United in the form of general histories, biographies, and autobiographies of players as well as statistical information. Clarke (1951) wrote an account of the club's history for a popular audience. Although it is not a 'serious' study it does contain some useful information about the club's early years.[8] Meek and Tyrrell (1997) have written a more substantial history of the club for the general reader. However, little mention is made in either book about the youth policy. Roberts (1975) has written a brief biographical account of the players who died at Munich. Although it is very sketchy, it contains some good oral testimony regarding the club's recruitment of young players.

The seminal history of the club is by Young (1960). He was the first to delve into the club's archives and produce a well-researched and erudite history of the club from its birth in 1878 to the end of our period. It is an important source because it gives a richly documented account of the origins of the club's youth policy. Green (1978) has written an updated version of Young's masterpiece which again is extremely well researched and written to mark the club's centenary.

SIR MATT BUSBY

It may come as a surprise that there have been few biographies about Sir Matt Busby given his eminence throughout the football world. Manchester United and Matt Busby are inextricably linked because it was he who resurrected the club after the war when the ground lay in ruins following German bombing raids. Glanville (1994) wrote an interesting tribute to Busby published the year of his death. It contains some very useful oral testimony from family members and former players which illuminate various facets of his life, including his establishment of a youth policy.

The two major biographies of Busby are Miller (1994) and Dunphy (1991). Miller is forthright in claiming from the outset that Busby was a revolutionary in his quest to produce his own players via a youth system. This at a time when other clubs continued to strengthen their teams by buying players. Busby was also a revolutionary in his approach to running a football club according to Dunphy. He asserts that Busby tried to instil 'family values' into the players. Like a family, a club had to treat its players with decency and respect - this would be repaid by improved performances on the field. Therefore, the club was more than just an academy: "but this was a home, a human place".

Busby's philosophy was exemplified by his insistence on donning a tracksuit to join in training with the players - he wanted to be close to them, developing a sense of camaraderie. Dunphy believes the reason for this was the loss of his father in the First World War.[9] This had left him vulnerable, unprotected and he wished to recreate his family at Manchester United. Busby was a sensitive man and sensitive to protect other people. This radical approach to working with his players was a long way from the hierarchical structure that prevailed in football clubs at the time, where day-to-day training was left to the coaches and the players only saw the manager on match days. In short, we were seeing the emergence of a 'new kind of manager'.

SAINT MATT:

HIS INTRODUCTION OF A SYSTEMATIC YOUTH POLICY WAS A FIRST FOR BRITISH FOOTBALL AND INFLUENCED CLUBS IN EUROPE AND BEYOND.

Dunphy's book is valuable because it provides the unusual perspective of a former player of the club in the early sixties.[10] Thus he had first hand experience of Busby's management style. Herbert Chapman and Major Frank Buckley had a similar impact on their respective clubs before the war at Arsenal, Huddersfield Town and Wolverhampton Wanderers. Dunphy examines the life of Busby from the standpoint of football reality (realpolitic) rather than idealism. He argues that Busby well understood the harsh reality that failure would ultimately mean dismissal from his job. He was a hard man, well versed in the requirements for football survival. He could be ruthless when necessary, but he preferred to show the velvet glove.[11]

THE YOUTH POLICY

This chapter concludes by looking specifically at the origins of Manchester United's youth policy. The principle of producing their own players had been stated in Manchester on a number of occasions notably in *The Manchester Guardian* in 1909 and by James Gibson, the Chairman, in 1931. The idea was to unite the junior and senior players at the club. At a Board meeting on 1st June 1937 it was decided to give special attention to the coaching of youth players. On 22nd February 1938 a further move was made, "with reference to the formation of a junior athletic club for cultivating young players after they leave school". At the club's AGM on 17th August 1938 Mr Gibson said the Manchester United Junior Athletic Club scheme (MUJAC) was being helped by a committee of teachers and instructors from the University of Manchester. This is interesting evidence of the club's collaboration with the academic world; a measure also of just how seriously the club were taking this new initiative.

By 1939 the scheme was flourishing - the junior team scoring 223 goals in winning the Chorlton League. The team included John Aston who was to become an England international. His son was to play a prominent part in the 1968 European Cup final in which United defeated Benfica to win the Cup for the first time. At the AGM in 1939 Mr Gibson again alluded to the scheme, proudly asserting that: "it was from these unusually comprehensive nurseries that the club hopes an all-Manchester team at some distant period will be produced" (Young 1960). It is interesting that thirty years later the club won the European Cup with eight players who had been developed by the youth scheme:

MANCHESTER UNITED SUMMER SCHOOL EXTRACT FROM THE MANCHESTER EVENING NEWS 15TH MAY 1952

"MANCHESTER UNITED ARE THE ONLY CLUB IN THE COUNTRY TO RUN A CLOSE-SEASON COACHING SCHOOL FOR THE DEVELOPMENT OF YOUTH. TONIGHT, THURSDAY, POSSIBLE STARS OF THE FUTURE GOT TOGETHER AT OLD TRAFFORD FOR A CHAT AND A CUP OF TEA WITH JIMMY MURPHY (ASSISTANT MANAGER AND COACH) AND BERT WHALLEY (COACH). AT THE WELCOME TONIGHT, TEA WAS SERVED TO THE LADS BY MRS ANN EVANS, ON RIGHT, THE CLUB STEWARDESS. WITH THE LADS ARE, LEFT, MR J ARMSTRONG (THE UNITED SCOUT WHO HAS HELPED TO FIND SOME OF THE LADS), JIMMY MURPHY (ASSISTANT MANAGER AND COACH) AND BERT WHALLEY (COACH) (CENTRE-FRONT) AND TRAINER BILL INGLIS (RIGHT REAR, WITH BALD HEAD) NOTE: COACHING PROPER BEGINS ON **TUESDAY NEXT.**"

Aston, Best, Brennan, Charlton, Foulkes, Kidd, Sadler and Stiles. Of these Aston, Brennan, Kidd and Stiles were born in Manchester.

It is clear then, that a youth policy was already in place before Busby arrived at the club in 1945. This was acknowledged by Busby himself. United, however, were not the only club interested in establishing a youth policy. Wolverhampton Wanderers, under the managership of Major Frank Buckley, had begun a programme of youth development as early as 1927.[12] Young says that Buckley's first job was not to buy but rather to 'make' players via a youth system. Like the Jesuits he believed in the merits of early instruction and he sought out boys in the Wolverhampton neighbourhood and taught them the fundamentals of the game. Buckley produced some outstanding players during his time at Wolves (1927-44), notably Stan Cullis and Billy Wright. Cullis was later to become the manager of Wolves and Wright went on to have a distinguished career, earning 105 caps for England, a record at the time.

Matt Busby became manager of Manchester United on 19th February 1945 with a five year contract and according to Young: "formulated a clear, decisive, progressive policy for his club". Success could only be assured by planning in depth - through the reserves to the juniors and youth teams. In his autobiography (1957) Busby asserts that from the day of his appointment a decision on youth policy had to be made. There was a concentrated campaign for youth development. He believed that Manchester United players had to be found as soon as they left school or in youth clubs. They would then develop and mature with the club and have a sense of loyalty to it: "I wanted to build teams of world-class footballers and to do the job efficiently had to get hold of them young - as soon as they were available, in fact". Thus, although Busby did not invent the concept of having a youth policy, in the words of Hopcraft: "more than any other manager he put his faith and reputation into it".

It is important to remember that Busby was implementing his revolutionary ideas at a time when the country was emerging from the rigours of war. Thus his rebuilding of the club both structurally and spiritually mirrored the rebuilding of the nation as a whole. The aftermath of the war was still being felt with food shortages everywhere and rationing still operating for a year or two. Arthur Marwick (1968) has described the period between 1945-1950 as: "a crepuscular zone with the shadows of night as firm upon the landscape as the heartening hints of the rising sun". Life in these years was dominated by the consequences of war. In football terms, however, there was a boom in attendances, but also a shortage of players which made a youth policy even more important.

There were also important cultural changes taking place in the early 1950s which saw the emergence of the 'Teddy Boy' as representative of working-class youth's detachment from Society. This formed the backdrop in which the youth players at the club were beginning their football careers. They would clearly need a good deal of self discipline in order to resist the various temptations youth culture was presenting.

Having reviewed some of the literature relevant to this study and placed Matt Busby's work in a particular social and football context, the next chapter will analyse his main method of procuring young players for the club - the scouting system.

NOTES

[1] Elias's favourite example is the fox hunt, in which the hunters no longer actually kill the fox themselves but rather they do their "killing by proxy" (Elias 1978), *An essay on sports and violence* in Elias and Dunning (Eds*) Quest for Enlightenment*.

[2] Changes in the laws of the game, eg the offside law, and tactical developments within the game affect the configurations on the field that are formed by the teams.

[3] Desmond Morris in *The Soccer Tribe* (1981) looks at many of these issues from the point of view of ethnomethodology.

[4] Aesthetics is an extremely complex subject which has strong philosophical overtones. It seeks to answer questions about the nature of beauty, and whether the terms beauty and aesthetics are interchangeable (Whiting and Masterson 1974).

[5] From boxing, cricket and football respectively.

[6] Matthews, Finney, Puskas, Di Stefano, Beckenbauer, Cruyff, Charlton, Pelé to name but a few.

[7] Hopcraft wrote for *The Observer* and *The Sunday Times*.

[8] Clarke was a journalist with the *Manchester Evening News*. He died in the 1958 Munich disaster.

[9] Busby's father was killed in Arras in 1916, an experience which had a profound affect on him.

[10] Dunphy is a highly respected football journalist working in Ireland. His book *Only a Game* (1986) is widely considered a classic of the genre.

[11] A man who could recover so well from a disaster like Munich must have had enormous inner strength and determination.

[12] Born in Lancaster, Buckley enlisted in the army aged 16 at the start of the Boer War. During the First World War he served with the 17th Battalion (1st Football) Middlesex Regiment and rose to the rank of Major (Young 1976).

**CHAPTER TWO:
THE SCOUTING
SYSTEM**

This chapter will trace the origins of scouting early this Century, before explaining how Manchester United, in particular, recruited young players directly from schoolboy football through their scouting network. It will examine the origin and structure of the scouting system especially the influential role of the chief scout Joe Armstrong who joined the club after the war. The scouting criteria will also be explained as well as the relationship between the club and the Manchester Schools Football Association (MSFA). Little is generally known about the recruitment and selection process at the club during the fifties and this chapter seeks to explore important aspects of what was an extremely successful system. Manchester United's youth policy depended on the 'quality' of the players coming into the club's programme. This is as true today as it was in the fifties.[1]

THE 1870 EDUCATION ACT had a profound effect on the development of schoolboy football during the last decades of the nineteenth century. After 1870 English towns had an education system which obviously drew local children to the schools. Boys were introduced to football through school teams and inter-school competitions. This developed into inter-town and inter-regional competitions and was a vital means of generating and maintaining interest in football among boys from working class families. Thus, by the end of the century thousands paid to watch finals of local schoolboy competitions played to win cups and medals.[2]

The 1890s saw organised schools football really taking shape although the English Schools Football Association (ESFA) was not formed until 1904. The ESFA is the governing body of schoolboy football in England. It was founded the same year as the Federation of International Football Associations (FIFA). Senior clubs often assisted schoolboy football and Preston North End offered a challenge shield for inter-school football as early as 1884-85. Leicester Fosse permitted the use of their ground for schoolboy matches, and 100 free season tickets for boys who played for school teams. Mason (1970) goes as far as asserting that many schoolboy players were being recruited by professional clubs as early as the 1880s and 90s.

This is confirmed by Colm Kerrigan in a paper published in the *International Journal of the History of Sport* entitled: *London Schoolboys and Professional Football 1899-1915* (August

1994). Schools football developed at such a fast pace that by 1928 six thousand schools belonged to the ESFA and this increased to eight thousand by 1949 the beginning of this study. One reason that football became so popular was the pyramid system which enabled an outstanding schoolboy player to play for his school, town, county, and ultimately England boys. This structure nurtured talent that first developed via street games.[3] Street games are the spontaneous games that children play without supervision, rules or any of the constraints organised sports place on them. This is the play element that Huizinga refers to in *Homo-Ludens* (1970) which will be discussed later in relation to coaching at the club.

We have seen that scouting for young talent was not a new phenomenon at the beginning of the fifties and Fishwick reports an instance before the war of a manager who was known to visit mining areas to get young talent. He thought that a career in football was better than working down the pit. Fishwick (1989) says that the attractiveness of professional football for working class men included: better pay, good working conditions and local or national recognition.[4] Schoolteachers were beginning to have an influential role - schoolteacher Neil Franklin had contacts with professional clubs and passed on information about good young players to them. He eventually became a professional footballer himself with Stoke City and England.

As we have seen in previous chapters, Matt Busby and Frank Buckley were seen to be the pioneers with regard to the harvesting of young talent and building nurseries for their development.[5] Busby asserts that he first thought about recruiting schoolboys when he was playing himself: "people often ask when I decided that the most important job was to attract and develop young players. The answer is that the importance of young players was at the back of my mind from the day I arrived at Manchester City as a youth player myself and was in digs with Jack Bray".[6] Busby believed he could sign the best young players from all over the country directly from school. This had two main purposes: the saving of expensive transfer fees and the opportunity to mould these young recruits in his own image and raise them the Busby way - the Manchester United way.

Busby believed passionately that if he could get boys early enough they could be trained according to some kind of pattern, a pattern he was trying to create at the club

JOE ARMSTRONG SUCCEEDED THE LEGENDARY LOUIS ROCCA, FOUNDER OF MUJACS, IN 1950. HERE, JOE WELCOMES NEW RECRUITS WITH TYPICAL BRIO.

As the signed photos show, Dennis Viollet (above), Bobby Charlton (right) and Duncan Edwards (over page) felt indebted to Joe Armstrong for their later successes.

from the first team through all the other teams. Therefore, if a boy graduated as far as his ability, attitude and courage could allow he would: "fit into the pattern without feeling like a stranger among people painting pretty pictures he did not understand and had never seen before" (Busby 1973). We will examine this theme later in greater detail in relation to life at Manchester United as a young player and the coaching and training programme.

In order to recruit the best schoolboys in the country staff selection was extremely important. For example, Jimmy Murphy was appointed Assistant Manager in 1945 with responsibility for the reserves and the assessment of schoolboys. The arrival of Joe Armstrong at the club after the war was a major coup for Busby - the last piece of the scouting jigsaw was now in place. Armstrong worked full time for the General Post Office (GPO) as an engineer and joined United from Manchester City where he came to know Busby as a player and the two became good friends.

It is a widely held view that Armstrong joined the club on the death of the Chief Scout, Louis Rocca, in 1950, but this is not true. In fact, his 'Scout Pass' which the author has had the privilege to see indicates that he was working for the club as early as 1947.[7] So with Busby and Murphy offering support whenever they could, Joe Armstrong came to play a pivotal role in developing a scouting system whose success became the envy of the football world. Joe Junior believes his father must have worked with Louis Rocca before his death. However, he is unsure of the precise nature of the relationship.

THE SCOUTING SYSTEM

It may come as a surprise that Manchester United did not have an elaborate scouting system during the fifties. Estimates of the number of scouts the club employed range from four or five to a maximum of eight. There were also three scouts based in Ireland which demonstrates how far the club were prepared to go in order to recruit the best boys. The three Irish scouts were: Bob Bishop, Bob Harper (Northern Ireland) and Billy Behan in Dublin. It was Bob Bishop who spotted the incomparable George Best playing in junior football in Belfast. Joe Lovejoy (1998) has written a splendid account of Best's football career. The task of the scouts was basically to scour the country and recruit the finest young schoolboys. It was the quality of the scouts that mattered, not the quantity.[8]

The organisation of the scouting was simple in that Joe Armstrong would make the first recommendation either himself or through information which came to him via the other scouts. This was then followed up by one of the senior staff.[9] Scouts had instructions to concentrate on boys and youths. They would watch them several times and then they were watched by Jimmy Murphy or Bert Whalley for another opinion.[10] Busby firmly believed that the qualities he was looking for in a player could only be found at schoolboy level. Scouting at the club was not a random process but rather the result of: "planning, hoping, organisation and sheer hard work". Busby's personal involvement was crucial. He was the central computer through whom information was fed. His strength was the ability to delegate responsibility to those whose judgement he trusted, whose work was to select only 'good apples'.

How then were the boys selected? What were the criteria? Jimmy Murphy has said that the scouts were looking for basic skill, innate instinct for the game and a genuine desire to want to play for Manchester United. Busby believed the scouts should look for ability, discipline, loyalty and clean living along with an enthusiastic enjoyment of the game. Players with these qualities would be the lifeblood of the kind of club he was trying to build.

JOE ARMSTRONG

The esteem in which Joe Armstrong was held within the game can be gauged by an article in the *Dublin Evening Herald* (10th January 1970) by Don Revie, the Manager of Leeds United. Revie had a tremendous amount of success with his Leeds United team of the late 1960s and early 1970s, winning two League championships and an FA Cup.[11] Revie said the following about him:

"Certainly, I doubt whether Manchester United would have enjoyed so much success in the last two decades but for the presence of a man who is a household name within the game but virtually unknown among the fans. He is Joe Armstrong, 76-year-old hero of United's remarkable scouting network."

Revie is quite right to say that little is generally known about Armstrong and his methods, but the following comments by his son offers a remarkable insight into the man:

"One of the key factors was that my father worked for the GPO. That gave him communication skills which were well advanced. Therefore, he could make good contacts and maintain those contacts. He was in his own way quite methodical, single minded - never a 'yes man'. He had an excellent memory. This helped him to identify the important things he needed to know. My father kept quite detailed reports on senior players. Schoolboy records were probably not quite as detailed although he probably kept some kind of record. My father would direct scouts to watch certain players in specific matches - he was the main link between the club and the scouts.

"The main contacts were the District Secretaries of the English Schools FA who were themselves teachers, and then within that he had a lot of contacts in the Manchester area. He used to swear by the telephone because contacts were easily made by phone. People used to write in to the club as well as perhaps the odd teacher. He found out what games were on and went to matches. Personal contact with individual teachers was important and he always seemed to do the right thing. For example, he would go through the proper channels whenever possible.

"Most of all he was trusted! The schoolboy structure was large so that the best boys usually end up playing for the Town, County and England Boys. My father thought the minor games, that is, Town games, were just as important as schoolboy internationals for scouting young talent.[12] My father was adept at sorting out difficult addresses and venues for matches because of his telephone knowledge and contacts within the GPO.

"He was persuasive, good in company and always charmed the mothers - made a bee-line for the mother. He always recognised that the mother was the key figure to win over.[13] He'd just be polite, interested in the family, a bit of a flatterer, a humorist but he was sincere, he did think about things. It wasn't just a front; he thought about what he'd promised.

"It used to hurt him if he felt he'd let somebody down. Running right through was the

feeling that he was a religious man and because of that the family was important. The welfare of kids was seen to be important. Bobby Charlton referred to my mum and dad as 'Auntie Sally and Uncle Joe'." INTERVIEW

It is interesting to note that Armstrong's work at the GPO gave him contacts that otherwise would have been difficult to establish. This was an enormous advantage and he made the most of it. Joe Junior mentions that his father was quite methodical and single minded - knowing exactly what he wanted and striving to achieve it. His memory and recall of details was obviously an important aspect of his success and it needed to be! I have seen extracts from his diaries and his reporting of matches and comments are extremely sketchy. This was probably due to the fact that scouts in general were reluctant to keep detailed records in case they were lost and fell into the wrong hands. Joe Junior said there was a lot of 'cloak and dagger stuff' going on.[14]

The following entry in his diary on 29th January 1955 is an example of the kind of recording he made: "fair game, good report - N Lawton Manchester Boys v Southport". The expression 'fair game' was very likely shorthand for noting in his 'memory bank' that Lawton was a good prospect without giving too much away. The N Lawton referred to in the diary was Nobby Lawton, who eventually made 44 appearances in United's first team. He moved on to Preston North End and captained them in the 1964 FA Cup final which they lost to West Ham United. The recruitment of the best young footballers for Manchester United obviously required covert operations from time-to-time if Armstrong was to be successful.

It seems clear from Joe Junior's testimony that scouting at the club was well organised under the supervision of his father. Miller (1994) states that three-quarters of the players recruited came from 'tip-offs' received from schoolmasters who had connections with the club or supporters. Green concurs, stating that schoolmasters played a part, seeing in United a good home for youngsters and a stepping stone to a career.

The signing of Duncan Edwards is an interesting case in point. Matt Busby received a 'tip' from Joe Mercer (later to become Manager of Manchester City) about him. Mercer at the time was in charge of the England Schoolboys team. The signing of Edwards was a major coup for United because he was the outstanding schoolboy talent of the era. In fact he played for England Boys for three consecutive years 1950-51-52, the only player ever

to do so. This was and remains quite an astonishing achievement. Another excellent example of this was the signing of Bobby Charlton.

Arthur Hopcraft, the distinguished sportswriter, tells the story of how Charlton came to sign for United. In a magazine article entitled *The Charlton Boys: Bobby and Jack*, in *London Weekend Television* magazine in 1968, Hopcraft says that Mr Stuart Hemingway, the Headmaster of a secondary school in Ashington, Northumberland, and a former teacher at Manchester Grammar School, wrote to the club advising them that Bobby was showing outstanding talent and they should send someone to watch him. Joe Armsmtrong duly saw him play for the first time on 9th February 1953 for East Northumberland Boys v Hebburn and Jarrow Boys at Hebburn. Armstrong was impressed and took immediate action. His 'single-mindedness' was evident in that he made a speedy approach to his mother and backed his judgement with an offer.[15]

It is notable that Armstrong approached Charlton's mother - the proper channels his son mentioned.[16] Notice also that Armstrong saw Charlton play in a 'Town' representative game because he went on to become a schoolboy international later in the year. By the time a boy got as far as England Boys, scouts from all over the country were trying to recruit them so the competition was enormous. Therefore, striking early was vital. Terry Beckett makes the following comment regarding Armstrong's shrewd approach to spotting good schoolboys:

> "He knew the players, the lads he wanted and he kept to the Town teams. I think a lot of that was because once a lad got to England Boys numerous clubs went after him. Whereas if he cops them at the Town teams it's like previous to what they [the opposition] might do... I never saw him at school matches, he kept mainly to Town games." INTERVIEW

Joe Junior comments on his father's personal qualities and Busby's description of him as a 'gentleman ferret' mean that Armstrong's personality formed a large part of his success. Terry Beckett makes the following observation:

> "He had a way of getting along with people and my father was always a little bit

fascinated about how Joe went about things, strangely enough. He used to say: 'and that scout who calls to the house, Joe Armstrong there's something about him...' My dad was quite impressed with him, I don't know why though. I think it was his personality - yes, definitely, he used to mention him quite frequently." INTERVIEW

This business of 'getting to know the mothers' that Joe Junior describes is intriguing, evoking a sense of the importance of family and kin. This theme will be picked up in the next chapter. There is proof that Armstrong got extremely close to the Charlton family because Cissie Charlton, Bobby's mother, went as far as writing a letter to him with the salutation: "to Uncle Joe".[17] Furthermore, Joe Junior has in his possession a photograph of Bobby wearing his full England Boys strip including cap and signed "Best wishes to Mr and Mrs Armstrong from Bobby Charlton". Joe Junior showed me a photograph of Dennis Viollet, one of his father's signings. Dennis was a schoolboy international who went on to play 259 league games for the club. In fact he still holds the club's league goalscoring record of 32 goals in 36 matches in season 1959-60. The photograph is signed: "To Joe with best wishes and thanks for everything, Dennis Viollet." Sadly, Dennis died in March 1999 following a long illness.

It is clear then that Joe Armstrong had a personality that endeared him to people, he was a charming and charismatic figure as well as being a good psychologist. These qualities enabled him to attract outstanding schoolboys to Manchester United in the fifties, such as Bobby Charlton, Duncan Edwards, Wilf McGuinness and David Pegg. All of them played for England Schoolboys. A measure of the affection that players had for Joe Armstrong is demonstrated by a postcard he received from Switzerland sent by Bobby Charlton and Wilf McGuinness long after they had joined the club. Charlton also presented a china plate to him to commemorate his 100 caps for England - there was a limited edition of 750 and Joe received number three. He also gave him an England cap awarded for a game against Romania in 1968. The author had the privilege to see this memorabilia during his interview with Joe Junior in November 1998.

How, then, did Manchester United attract boys from the North East (Charlton), Midlands (Edwards) and Eire (Whelan) which were long distances for a 15-year-old boy to go in those days before the benefits of modern communications and transport.[18] Bobby Charlton offers the following reason for joining the club: "I felt that if I could make it at

United I could make it anywhere, it was as simple as that. It was a challenge and I never lived to regret it". In an interview he gave to David Miller for *The Sunday Telegraph* (2nd April 1973) Charlton gave the following reason for joining Manchester United:

> *"I signed for Manchester United, and not Newcastle or anyone else, mainly because of that wonderful little man Joe Armstrong, their Chief Scout. He's watched me long before I was in any schoolboy internationals, and he always said he wanted me to come and play for United, not to come for trials. Besides United were just starting to put youngsters into the first team, which was unheard of, and the idea of going to Old Trafford was exciting. The first thing you realised was that it was a family club."* INTERVIEW

Busby has said that in the case of Duncan Edwards it was "his burning desire to play for United" that attracted him. Miller also recounts a story of Edwards being hauled from his bed during the early hours to sign - such was the competition for his signature. Wilf McGuinness has said that the reason he joined United was that having watched the youth team play in the FA Youth Cup against Wolves (winning 7 - 1) he decided that: "if they can do that for players who haven't turned out for England, what can they do for me who has captained England". McGuinness was referring to Eddie Colman and Albert Scanlon respectively, who had not gone on to play for England schoolboys. Terry Beckett offers an extremely perceptive opinion on why United attracted the top schoolboys in the country:

> *"Well, there were various clubs I could have gone to but I would say that United stood out because of their youth policy just prior to when I went to United and the fact that so many young players were given the opportunity in the first team, and obviously you fancied being one of them. I plumped for United because the young lads were being given their chances. That had a big influence on it."*[19] INTERVIEW

Having examined the evidence it seems that the primary motivation for young boys to join United was fourfold: a desire to join a major club; a feeling that the club's youth policy would improve them as players; an early opportunity to play for the first team, and the fact that Manchester United was a family club. Obviously, there was competition from other clubs and Cissie Charlton says that 18 clubs were trying to sign Bobby, offering all kinds of inducements including one of £800, a considerable sum in those days. So it is clear that financial and other inducements were being offered to boys by clubs and if, as several newspapers have claimed over the years, United offered inducements to sign players, they were not alone.

Terry Beckett claims that Stan Cullis, the Wolves Manager, had visited his home on two separate occasions to try and recruit him. He came on his own by train and taxi such was his desperation. Cullis was no doubt still annoyed that United had stolen Duncan Edwards from under his nose and was probably trying to exact revenge. Terry also had in his possession a letter to his parents dated 26th October 1953 from Arthur Rowe, the Tottenham Hotspur Manager. He had seen him playing in London for Manchester Boys against London Boys at White Hart Lane, Spurs' Ground. He was writing to ask them to consider allowing Terry to join them. This personal letter from the manager of a rival for his signature is compelling evidence of the level of competition among professional clubs for top schoolboy footballers. This makes Armstrong's achievements all the more remarkable. Moreover, Armstrong never drove and relied entirely on trains or taxis to travel around the country.

THE MANCHESTER SCHOOLS FA

The Manchester Schools FA was formed in 1889 and has been the governing body of schools football in the city right up to today. Both Manchester clubs, City and United, have been patrons of the Association for many years offering support in a variety of ways, including the use of their grounds for major matches.[20] Over the years Manchester United have had much success signing local boys who have played for Manchester Boys; Dennis Viollet, Wilf McGuinness and Nobby Stiles being outstanding examples from the fifties.

The relationship between the Manchester Schools FA and Manchester United seems to have been reciprocal during the fifties and continues to be today. They would help each other whenever they could although the Schools FA remained fiercely independent from the professional clubs in matters of policy and procedures. For example, the MSFA handbooks 1948-1955 have no advertising relating to either United or City. Any advertising is primarily for sports shops, coach firms or milk and drink companies. It is not until the handbook of 1956-57 that anything directly related to professional football appears. Page 51 of the booklet contains an advertisement: "A message to schoolboy readers from Manchester United". It refers to an offer of free admission to reserve matches at the club at the request of schools. The MSFA also published a monthly 'bulletin' during the fifties and little mention is made of either of the professional Mancunian clubs. However, there is one reference to a charity match between Manchester Boys and Salford Boys on 27th September 1950 at Manchester United's ground. Proceeds were to go to the Newsvendors Benevolent Fund. This shows that the MSFA and the club co-operated in support of local charities. What is interesting, however, is the lack of evidence that Manchester Boys played any competitive matches as Old Trafford on a regular basis. The evidence points to many 'high profile' Manchester Boys games which were played at Maine Road, perhaps evidence that the MSFA did not want to be too closely linked with either club.[21] It is notable, also, that each of the handbooks contain the fixtures for both United and City for the current season.

What, then, was the nature of the relationship between Joe Armstrong and the MSFA? Terry Beckett has the following to say in this regard:

> *"He had contact with teachers - what information was passed on I don't know. You got teachers who were United supporters and they would be over the moon for their lad to go there as in Mr Mulligan's case where Nobby, myself and Brian Kidd went from St Patrick's."* INTERVIEW

The 'Mr Mulligan' Terry refers to was a teacher at St Patrick's in Collyhurst, Manchester, who had close links with the MSFA. Both Nobby Stiles and Brian Kidd (European Cup Winners, 1968) went to 'St Pat's', a school which had a wonderful tradition of producing outstanding footballers. Mr Mulligan was a United supporter and Joe Armstrong, wily as he was, used contacts like this with school teachers for the benefit of Manchester United. Furthermore, Laurie Cassidy has the following to say about the relationship between the MSFA and the club:

> *"It was always if they could help the Manchester Schools FA with such things as if one of the boys got injured they would look after them, give them treatment at the Cliff...*

I think if I'm not mistaken there used to be occasions when they would autograph footballs for raffles and so on." INTERVIEW

Terry Beckett corroborates the fact that Manchester Boys players received treatment for injuries. He remembered the selectors sending him to Old Trafford for treatment.

It appears from the above that relations between the club and the MSFA were cordial and mutually beneficial. Joe Armstrong and his team of scouts had good contacts with teachers who were themselves involved with the MSFA. This afforded easy access to officials to glean information about players. The MSFA benefited by using the facilities of the club to have injured players looked after as well as receiving assistance with fund raising.

We have seen that scouting for boys had roots at the end of the 19th century and scouting became more systematic as professional clubs saw the benefits of signing boys straight from school. Manchester United, through the vision of Matt Busby, devoted a great deal of time and commitment to recruiting the best schoolboy players with the aim of getting them into the first team. Joe Armstrong, the Chief Scout, was instrumental in the process with his scouting methods and 'cult of personality'. Schoolboys were attracted to the club because it had a good youth policy, providing youngsters with the opportunity to test themselves at the highest level. The fact that United, through Joe Armstrong, presented themselves as a 'family club' was also a motivating factor. Relations between the club and the MSFA were good and this served the interests of both parties.

We have seen how the boys were recruited and how they have committed themselves to joining the club. The route of progression through the club from schoolboy star to first team player is the subject of the next chapter.

NOTES

[1] Almost every professional club in the Country has a scouting network and generally the bigger the club the bigger the network.

[2] Football has always been seen as a working class game, although this is changing with the modern day commercialisation of the sport, see Walvin (1975), Fishwick (1989) and Mason (1980).

[3] This system still prevails today although the County team no longer exists. However, most schoolboys and their parents still consider it a considerable honour to be selected to play for England Boys.

[4] Fishwick says that in 1947 players were earning twelve pounds during the season and ten in the close season. This salary was high when compared to working class averages (Fishwick 1989, p74).

[5] Ironically, one of Buckley's prodigies at Wolves, Stan Cullis, became one of Busby's main rivals in recruiting schoolboy players in the fifties.

[6] Manchester City was Busby's first professional club. He was in their 1934 FA Cup winning team when they defeated Portsmouth 2 - 1. It is notable also that even then Busby was sensitive to the plight of young footballers. Perhaps coloured by his own experience as a young player at Manchester City living far from home.

[7] His son, Joe Junior, had possession of several of his father's 'Scout Passes' which pre-date 1950. Notably his passes for seasons 1946-47 and 1947-48.

[8] Bob Harper and Billy Behan were responsible for signing Jackie Blanchflower and Billy Whelan respectively. Both players went on to make significant contributions to the pre-Munich team as well as becoming internationals. Whelan tragically died at Munich (Dykes 1994).

[9] Busby in his autobiography said that he and Jimmy Murphy searched for young players constantly - often together (1973, p23).

[10] Bert Whalley was a former player who joined the coaching staff after his career ended through injury. He was to die at Munich. We will discuss him in more detail in Chapters Three and Four.

[11] Revie's Leeds were one of the most successful teams of the 1970s.

[12] eg Manchester or Liverpool Boys.

[13] This differs from modern-day scouting where the tendency is to try and win over the father.

[14] Joe Junior has told the author that his father would often do and ask questions later. It was suggested to him that his father was probably a 'loveable rogue' and he did not disagree.

[15] Joe Junior uses the word 'singleminded' to refer to his father's decisiveness and purpose of intent.

[16] It seems that directly approaching young boys was frowned on and scouts usually spoke to staff before approaching a boy's parents. Joe Junior had told the author that following protocol was extremely important so as not to upset school staff which could hinder their access to boys. Furthermore, a boy could not actually sign for a club until he had left school. See Chapter Three.

[17] The letter was written in 1953.

[18] A reasonable modern comparison would be a sixteen-year-old boy going to France or Italy to join a club.

[19] Beckett cites players like Jeff Whitefoot and Dennis Viollet who made their League debuts as teenagers. In the case of Whitefoot he is probably the youngest player to appear in the first team, making

his debut aged just 16 against Portsmouth, 15th April 1950, (Dykes 1994).

[20] The Manchester Boys team have use of the club's indoor facilities at the Cliff, Lower Broughton, Salford for training, particularly during the Winter months.

[21] Terry Beckett says that he can't remember playing any Manchester Boys Games at Old Trafford. The MSFA Handbook 1955-56 has a photograph action during a match between Manchester Boys and Sunderland at Maine Road, Manchester City's ground (p33).

**CHAPTER THREE:
THE YOUTH
SYSTEM**

"I did not set out to build a team: the task ahead was much bigger than that. What I really embarked upon was the building of a system which would produce not one team but four or five, each occupying a rung of the ladder the summit of which was the First XI." MATT BUSBY

ONCE THEY HAVE been recruited from schoolboy football, the players began their journey through the club's junior teams. This chapter tries to show how the youth structure was organised and what it was actually like to be a youth player at Manchester United during the fifties. The degree of success achieved by the youth programme will also be analysed. The chapter will describe the various leagues the juniors played in as well as the actual playing conditions they experienced. A comparison will be made with modern day youth development at professional clubs, such as centres of excellence and football academies which were established in 1998. When compared to modern methods of youth development the question of the quality of education the youth players at the club received during the fifties will also be discussed. The chapter will explain the distinction between being on the groundstaff at the club or working fulltime for local firms in order to learn a trade. Some players continued to attend school and college and this raised various issues regarding working conditions and contractual arrangements.

Important aspects of the players' social life, including their living arrangements, will be described and analysed, as well as the ways in which the club was able to exercise a measure of control over them through the official club rules. The notion that Matt Busby actively sought to create a 'family club', instilling a sense of loyalty, belonging, respect and attachment of the players to each other and the club will be explored. In this regard, the chapter seeks to analyse to what extent the club's ethos was a reflection of Busby's wider political and social beliefs - his socialism - germinating from his upbringing in a Scottish mining village in which family and community were important values. Elias and Dunning's (1971) configurational sociology will be discussed briefly in relation to issues of rivalry and competition between the players.

THE JUNIOR PLAYING STRUCTURE

We have seen that when Matt Busby became Manager of Manchester United in 1945, the Manchester United Junior Athletic Club (MUJAC) was already a well-established programme for the development of youth. Busby had the sagacity to refrain from tampering with a system which had already produced outstanding players such as John Aston, who went on to make 282 appearances in the first team and play 17 times for England. The MUJAC system was the foundation on which Busby graduated his young schoolboy signings through the club's various junior teams, leading ultimately to the first team, the summit of a player's achievement.

Before the Second World War, the basic MUJAC system bequeathed to Busby comprised young players organised in the following age bands, according to Young (1960):

TEAM	AGE
'B' Team	15½ - 16½
'A' Team	16½ - 17½
'Colts' Team	17½ - 18½
Official 'A' Team	18½ - 20

This, then, was the framework on which the United youth system was built. Busby's idea was to maintain this 'layer of teams', each moving up the scale so that the basic MUJAC model remained relatively unchanged throughout the period of the study. By the end of the fifties, Busby (1957) described the following youth structure at Manchester United which included all youth footballers:

TEAM	LEAGUE
First Team	Football League Division 1
Reserves	Central League
Third Team	Lancashire League 'A' Division
Fourth Team	Lancashire League 'B' Division
Fifth Team	Eccles & District League

It is clear, then, that during the fifties Manchester United had a playing structure which enabled them to have five teams representing them on Saturdays. The younger reader may be surprised to learn that most aspiring professionals, that is boys as young as fifteen years of age, started their careers playing open-age football - football without any restrictions with regard to the age of the players. In practice, this meant that a boy as young as fifteen or sixteen could play in a match containing players ten, fifteen, or even twenty years older than himself. This is far removed from what is deemed to be acceptable in modern youth development programmes such as football academies, where, according to *The FA Premier League Rules, Section M, Youth Development 1998* players are restricted from playing against opposition more than two years older than themselves for health and safety reasons. There is a contradiction here, however, because age restrictions only apply at the junior levels of the game. There are no age restrictions in the Football Association Premier League or other senior leagues. Indeed, on 17th January 1999 Joe Cole, a seventeen-year-old, made his Premiership debut for West Ham United against Manchester United at Old Trafford. Therefore, age restrictions apply only in youth leagues, a situation which has a long legacy.[1]

Throughout the fifties Manchester United junior teams played in the following leagues: Altrincham, Eccles, Manchester, Manchester Amateur and Lancashire. They were all local leagues and apart from the Lancashire League, which included professional clubs, teams consisted of works or boys' club teams. This again is in contrast to modern football academies which are elite to the extent that they are only permitted to play matches against other academies. It is believed that this will help to raise standards. Any concept of playing against works or boys' clubs teams would be considered detrimental, indeed harmful, for a young player's development. What, then, was it actually like to play in these junior leagues in the fifties? Albert Scanlon, who joined Manchester United as an amateur in 1950 describes his initial baptism as a junior player at the club:

> *"So I started in the Juniors and they were in the Eccles League... you would play against men, it was open age, a lot of works' teams. You'd play against teams like Adelphi Lads' club which was open age, you'd play against teams like Brindle Heath, Kersal Lads..."* INTERVIEW

Frank Hannah, a youth referee during the fifties concurs, stating that Manchester United junior players:

> *"Weren't generally as physically strong as the teams they were playing because it was*

open age. Most of the teams, particularly with the colts, it was open age players they were playing against - some had been playing for years and had developed as men, whereas the young lads from Manchester United were in the teams and not physically developed. And, of course, there wasn't the physical training and development of youth that goes on now in those days. So what they lacked in strength they made up for in ability, team organisation and discipline." INTERVIEW

Bobby Charlton has recalled the early days of his football career at Manchester United following his arrival in 1953 when he was just fifteen years old. He has said that it was extremely difficult at first playing in tough leagues against local works teams like Avros, Ferranti and Miles Platting. Their sole objective was to beat a Manchester United team and often hundreds of workers would be on the touchline shouting and urging the United players to make a mistake. Frank Hannah has said during interview that it was an extremely high profile game when teams played Manchester United and: "to come and beat Manchester United Colts or one of the junior teams or even the 'A' team was an achievement". An example of the importance of games involving United is demonstrated by the fact that their opponents would often produce a programme for the match. The Manchester United Museum contains a programme of a match between Newton Heath Loco and Manchester United 'A' played on 19th August 1950 at Ceylon Street, Clayton. It was a fixture in the Manchester League. Newton Heath is in north Manchester, the place where the club was founded. Clayton is a mere kilometre away.

On reflection, however, Charlton believed that these experiences had benefits for his football education:

"It was a great atmosphere to be brought up in and it toughened me up considerably so that when I went into the Central League side, really my first taste of the professional game, I was ready for it." [2]

He remembers playing in the Manchester Amateur League:

"You were sixteen and this was open age football with big dockers and guys from factory teams kicking lumps out of you. But it was another fantastic education." (DUNPHY 1991)

Charlton believed this was a positive experience because some of the games were won by high scores: Eighteen or twenty goals a game helped build confidence and assurance:

> *"This is where brilliance could be expressed without fear of losing. That was important, a way of gaining confidence, of exploring the limits of your talent."*

The concept of "exploring the limits of your talent" is a feature of Huizinga's (1970) theory of play which we examined in Chapter One. Huizinga believed that you could only explore the extent of your talent if you were allowed to experiment without undue restrictions being placed on you. The idea of "discovery of experiential learning" is also encouraged within modern educational methodology.[3]

Wilf McGuinness believed this was a good football education because playing against teams of inferior ability, even if stronger physically, and winning by large margins helped instil confidence. All the junior players went through this process and the best ones survived due to their sheer talent - including Bobby Charlton. It is worth comparing this method with that of the Hungarian National Team, the Olympic Champions of 1952 who famously defeated England at Wembley the following year. They often prepared for major matches by playing against inferior opponents and winning by big scores which their coach Gusztav Sebes thought built confidence and helped ease tension (Taylor and Jamrich 1997).

Albert Scanlon has said that he had not realised at the time just what a good education all this was:

> *"Someone coming along and kicking you and giving you a dig, you'd never been used to it in your life... everyone wants to beat you and it was always physical."*

Frank Hannah, a shrewd observer, makes the following comment regarding the quality of football education playing in the local leagues gave United's young players:

> *"At the lower age of football the regulations now state a man can't or a boy can't play against a player more than two years (older) than himself because of the physical development.[4] I think that in the days we've been talking about Bobby Charlton that sort of era and before him, I think it must have been an experience. I mean if*

you think of the players that have played in the 'A' team and so forth: Dennis Viollet, Goodwin, Whitefoot and Pegg and those sort of players they all came through to the team so the experience and the training they were getting must have been good." [5]

Frank's reflections are valuable because they offer a neutral perspective. His comments regarding the current regulations and age restrictions for young players because of physical development stages is enlightening, making a sharp distinction between youth development today and accepted practice in the fifties. However, he asserts unequivocally that the fifties produced some outstanding footballers which is evidence that the football education they were receiving playing in these leagues had a large degree of merit. It could be argued football was more physical in the fifties in terms of contact, thus developing a young player's toughness and durability was a necessity. But we should be wary of turning a necessity into a virtue.

Perhaps we do not need to condition players in this way any more because the game has changed. For example, the modern game does not permit tackling from behind. Regarding this point, it is worth noting that Manchester United gave at least one teenager his Football League debut in each year before the crash. This is a remarkable achievement in an age when playing young players in the first team was considered revolutionary. The players were as follows: Birkett (1950); Blanchflower (51); Doherty (52); Edwards (53); Scanlon (54); McGuinness (55); Charlton (56); Dawson (57).

This structure enabled the club to produce one of the youngest sides ever to win the

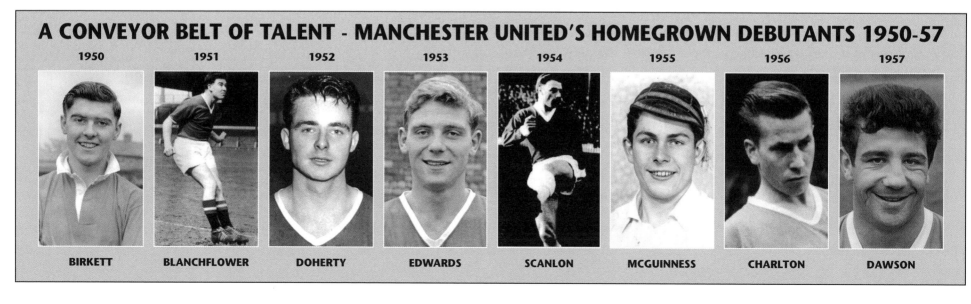

A CONVEYOR BELT OF TALENT - MANCHESTER UNITED'S HOMEGROWN DEBUTANTS 1950-57

1950	1951	1952	1953	1954	1955	1956	1957
BIRKETT	BLANCHFLOWER	DOHERTY	EDWARDS	SCANLON	MCGUINNESS	CHARLTON	DAWSON

championship in 1956. All but three of the players were developed by the club's youth system. The team had changed considerably from the one that had won the championship in 1952 which is a measure of how successful the youth programme had become.[6] It is important to keep in mind that Bobby Charlton was a graduate of the system and he went on to make 752 appearances in United's first team. He also played 106 times for England helping them to win the World Cup in 1966. One wonders what players like Colman, Edwards, Whelan and Pegg would have achieved if they had not been so tragically killed at Munich.

Even in the light of the sophistication of modern youth development with the emphasis on sports science,[7] it is difficult to criticise a system which produced such outstanding players even though it was far removed from modern day practice where health and safety and child protection factors have such a high profile. Charlton himself believed the system he came through was good. Playing in the Lancashire League, which was formed in the mid-fifties where professional club's junior teams played each other was, according to Charlton (1967), a much softer process.

INFAMOUS AMONG UNITED PLAYING STAFF, THE MATCHES PLAYED IN THE CAR PARK BEHIND THE STRETFORD END WERE RECKONED TO SORT THE WHEAT FROM THE CHAFF.

PLAYING CONDITIONS

The Manchester United junior teams travelled to some games by bus: a corporation bus, according to Albert Scanlon.[8] A coach was only used for 'A' or reserve team matches. The standard of playing pitches varied from being very good to extremely poor and this would obviously affect the standard of play. Frank Hannah offers the following description of typical playing conditions:

"One of the best areas to play football in those days was Eccles where they had the Cleavley Playing Fields which was a big expanse of field that was well-maintained. But a lot of the grounds that you played in that were maintained by the Local Authorities were not of that standard, although I believe they were better maintained than they are now. And if you're going to play football you need a good standard of pitch. Some of the pitches they had to play on were a bit rough." INTERVIEW

The crucial point that Frank Hannah makes is that in order to play football to a high standard a 'good standard' of pitch is required. This is as true today as it was in the fifties. We can see from the evidence presented that some of the grounds were sub-standard and this was detrimental to the production of quality football. 'Rough pitches', with muddy, uneven surfaces suited the physical style of play of opposing teams, on the other hand the young Manchester United players would have to be both physically and mentally alert in order to avoid lunging tackles. The uneven bounce of the ball helped refine technique and assisted their general development physically, technically and psychologically.

A graphic example of the playing conditions which the youth players endured is recounted wonderfully by Albert Scanlon who offers the following account of playing his first match for one of the junior teams circa 1950:

"And we all got on a bus and Bert Fishburn got the twelve, fourteen fares and just had two or three bags. You all carried your own boots and shin pads. And we got off at a place called Hans Renolds and that was in Burnage and was a big engineering works and nobody knew where we was going.[9] And we was all stood around and then Bert said 'follow me' and we walked down a path at the side of Hans Renolds and we just kept going and going and must have been about a mile down this path.[10] On the left hand side we appeared at a football field and it was fenced off - your ground had to be fenced off - and there was a fellow in the field at the side and he was tending pigs. And a few of the lads were now laughing. And one or two said to him 'what is this?' He said, 'it's a football pitch I rent it out' - he said 'it's mine - I'm a pig farmer'. And the ground was surrounded by pigs and the stink and the smell was awful. And that was United's home ground in the Eccles League and it was in the middle of a pig farm in Burnage." INTERVIEW

This account demonstrates quite convincingly how difficult it must have been for the players to perform at their optimal level given the inadequacy of some of the pitches they had to play on. Nevertheless, as we have seen, many of them had the mental strength and physical courage to endure these tests and graduate to the first team. A quite remarkable achievement when a comparison is made with the facilities available at the club today. Of course, the most talented players such as Bobby Charlton and Duncan Edwards

A TYPICAL OUTING FOR UNITED'S YOUTH TEAM

progressed through the junior teams on merit. The general philosophy then, as now, is that if a player is good enough, age should not be a barrier to progress.

WORKING CONDITIONS

In his autobiography, Busby (1973) said that regarding the well-being of the boys he brought to the club from school, it would have been immoral for him as Manager to encourage parents to allow their sons to join the club without assuming full responsibility for their welfare. In this sense he became a surrogate father, believing that parents had to see that he really cared about them. Busby thought the two years between fifteen and seventeen were formative because what happened in this period determined whether they signed as full professionals with the club or otherwise. Therefore, he felt that: "if they were to acquire anything from Old Trafford I was determined it would not be bitterness". It should be stated that Busby had more than a moral responsibility for the boys, in some cases he had a legal one also. For example Jackie Blanchflower, who was to become an international for Northern Ireland, came to the club in 1949. The regulations required that due to his age he had to have a legal guardian before he could leave Ireland. Busby duly signed the necessary documents. He clearly had to take this responsibility seriously.

Busby believed that there was much more to the development of young players than physical and technical training, they had to be properly housed and cared for by people who were prepared to make them part of their own families. They had to learn how to look after their finances and use their spare time constructively. The club found them work or put them on courses to learn a trade which would stand them in good stead if they failed to make the grade. Furthermore, if a boy did not make the grade Busby believed his parents should be properly informed which required sensitivity and was not an easy task. On the other hand, it was very fulfilling to see a young player coming through the system so that: "the foster father can join in with the parents and say 'that's my boy'." This broadly was Busby's philosophy with regard to the welfare of his young charges, but how did it work in practice?

It must be kept in mind that unlike today when clubs can sign boys as young as nine

LAPPING THE PITCH HAS BEEN A STAPLE OF A FOOTBALLER'S TRAINING SINCE THE GAME WAS INVENTED. HERE EDDIE COLMAN AND CO. ARE PUT THROUGH THEIR PACES.

years old, during the fifties a promising boy could not sign for a club until he had actually left school.[11] On leaving school he could sign only as an 'amateur' player so he received no pay, only legitimate expenses. A boy could not sign full professional forms until he was seventeen years of age. Therefore, a two-year vacuum had to be filled between fifteen and seventeen when he was eligible to sign full professional forms.[12] An aspiring professional footballer could fill this void in three basic ways: he could stay on at school or college and gain academic or vocational qualifications or get a job or learn a trade as an apprentice or join the groundstaff at the club. We shall now examine each of these options in turn.

Bobby Charlton is an excellent example of the first two options. On signing for Manchester United in 1953 Charlton had been attending Bedlington Grammar School in his native Ashington, Northumberland and his mother wanted him to continue his education. On coming to Manchester, he enrolled at Stretford Grammar School with Joe Armstrong's assistance, went to school during the day and trained with the club at night.[13] Needless to say, such a demanding schedule left him exhausted and he could not keep up with his schoolwork. He struggled on for a while, not wishing to offend either his mother or Joe Armstrong until the situation reached crisis point when he was selected to play for the school team one Saturday morning. This would have meant him playing two games in one day: for school in the morning and Manchester United in the afternoon. This was untenable. Charlton spoke to his mother and they agreed he should go and see the headmaster and inform him that he wished to concentrate on his football career. Because he was still only an amateur this meant he had to get a job or join the club's groundstaff which Charlton describes as a "a job in the loosest possible sense". Eventually, he took a job with an engineering firm for two pounds a week. He describes this as a waste of time, but it satisfied his family and eased his conscience. Charlton merely went through the motions at his 'trade' and never did any skilled work. (CHARLTON, 1967)

However, this was no easy option because the working day was long. He would rise at seven to begin work at eight in the morning. Work finished at five thirty and on two nights a week he trained at the club. Charlton came to envy the groundstaff players who strolled to work at nine thirty and finished at four. Many players took jobs in this way including Duncan Edwards (joiner), Bill Foulkes (collier) and Wilf McGuinness who took a job with a textile company.

The third option was to join the groundstaff which involved doing various jobs at the football ground for which you received a salary. The attraction of this option was the fact that you spent all of your time 'at the club' either working or watching the professionals train. You did this until you reached seventeen and became eligible to sign full professional forms. Albert Scanlon gives the following account of a typical day as a member of the groundstaff, circa, 1950:

"My first job was painting the ground. They gave us a five gallon drum of red oxide, a paint brush, and they said go out and paint everything red. Then, when we'd painted everything red, they'd come back with a drum of white and a different bucket and give you that and you'd go out and paint everything white that was white. You never sort of got involved in anything else but just Old Trafford as it was then. We did all the odd jobs. We'd sweep. You see there was such a lot of building work going on. They were building a stand - a firm called Woods was building the first stand you know after the war.[14] That was at Old Trafford. And you'd clean up. And then there was an old gym outside the dressing rooms and the only thing in the gymnasium was mats, big square mats and two medicine balls and a few weights. And Ted Dalton, the physiotherapist, he had his treatment room in there and every day, Monday to Friday, we swept and locked it and that was the job I finished with. And you were covered in dirt, dust - the water was rotten. All it was - it kept you there and you could train and we trained Tuesday and Thursday." INTERVIEW

ROGER BYRNE, ONE OF BUSBY'S EARLY RECRUITS THROUGH THE YOUTH SYSTEM, DEMONSTRATES THE GYM FACILITIES UNDER THE OLD TRAFFORD MAIN STAND

Judging from Scanlon's account, being "on the groundstaff" was not a glamorous option. The main incentive for being on the groundstaff was the day-to-day involvement at the heart of the club, "it kept you there". This was special because it was the next best thing to being a real professional. The money was good: three pounds, ten shillings a week according to Scanlon, when his father was earning two pounds, ten shillings. Scanlon remembers Bobby Charlton coming to the club and wishing to join the groundstaff simply because he wanted to be involved in football all day. He says:

"It gave you nothing because Bill Inglis gave you nothing. I don't think you got cocky." [15]

Rather surprisingly, Busby believed that groundstaff work was genuine work, and he secured jobs for players who did not wish to join the groundstaff through businessmen who were friendly towards the club. Thus it can be seen that the vacuum that had to be filled between the age of fifteen and seventeen could be filled in these distinct ways.

As an amateur player you did not have to commit yourself to the professional game, but Busby insisted that professional contracts were not offered at seventeen unless: "I am thoroughly satisfied that he is good enough". He did not believe in telling players they would reach the top and then discard them after twelve months. This was "immoral and unfair" to both the boy and his parents. On the other hand it was unfair to pressurise players to sign professional before they were ready because it might not be in their best interest. For example Busby wished to sign Reg Holland and Mark Pearson who had both reached seventeen and were eligible to sign professional. He delayed signing them because they wanted to play for the England Amateur team and signing professional would render them both ineligible. He respected their wishes and they eventually signed some time later: "the delay did me no harm, yet it did them some good" was his observation. Pearson went on to make eighty first team appearances for the club before being sold to Sheffield Wednesday for twenty thousand pounds in 1963. Thus Busby was duly rewarded for his patience and sensitivity in what was an extremely delicate situation.

Professional footballers in the fifties did not earn the large salaries of players today. Green (1978) states that following the threat of a strike in 1946 under the Professional Footballers' Association (PFA), Chairman Jimmy Guthrie oversaw a gradual increase in players' wages. However, increases in wages were generally slow and agitation by the union led ultimately to the abolition of the maximum wage in 1961-62. A typical salary in 1951 was fourteen pounds during the playing season which had only increased to seventeen pounds by 1957. A perusal of Bobby Charlton's contract in 1955 (Manchester United Museum archives) shows he was earning as little as seven pounds a week during the season. Duncan Edwards earned more as an established first team player, but this was only fifteen pounds a week. It is clear that professional footballers were not attracted to the game for financial gain even allowing for pre-inflationary times. The attraction of professional football was rather the excitement and challenge of striving to get to the top of the profession, and playing in front of crowds of sixty thousand people every week.

LIVING ARRANGEMENTS

An important aspect of the players' welfare was their living arrangements. Busby realised that when young boys came to the club from all over the country (see Chapter Two) they needed to be properly cared for. Therefore, he brought together a cadre of landladies to create a home away from home for them. A typical example of this policy was Mrs Watson's. She ran a boarding house at five Birch Avenue which was near Lancashire County Cricket Ground, not far from Old Trafford. The boarding house consisted of two large houses knocked into one which meant she could cater for up to twenty lodgers. The house was also used by commercial travellers and lorry drivers from time to time: "it was a relaxed, warm place" according to Dunphy (1991). June Jones, the wife of Mark Jones who died at Munich, recalls Bobby Charlton, Duncan Edwards, David Pegg and Tommy Taylor all resided there at one time or another.[16] Jimmy Murphy, Busby's assistant for over twenty-five years, has said that both he and Busby believed that the quality of the boys living accommodation (digs) was important:

TEA AT MRS WATSON'S: BUSBY FELT THAT HIS YOUNG PLAYERS SHOULD BENEFIT FROM A 'HOME AWAY FROM HOME' DURING THEIR APPRENTICESHIPS WITH THE CLUB.

> *"The club had a lot of houses which had been vetted and approved where the club knew the landladies were homely and motherly types."* (MURPHY 1968)

Both men knew the hardships of leaving home to live in a strange city far from their family and friends so they worked hard to make sure that the landladies had the right character and personality to look after these lively, vibrant and ambitious teenagers. Writing in 1968, Murphy says that many of them had served the club loyally for twenty years. Thus it can be seen that Busby did all he could to make sure that when they were away from work or the club they had a happy, settled home life which would help their progress as aspiring professional footballers.

A FAMILY CLUB

Cliff Lloyd, the former Chairman of the Professional Footballers' Association, was a colleague of Matt Busby when they played for Liverpool in 1938. Even then he saw in Busby qualities that endeared him to young players:

> *"Matt was a man young players would go to if they had any problems. Even then he was interested in the younger players."* (ROBERTS 1975)

Les Olive, a former player, Secretary and later club Director, remembers Busby's arrival at the club in 1945.[17]

> *"He wanted it to be a family club and he played his part in making it that way by showing an interest in people, so that everybody was important. He used to say that we don't have first team players and second and fourth team players - they're all Manchester United Players."* (GLANVILLE 1994)

It has been argued that Busby wanted to recreate at Manchester United the close family and community he had experienced in the small mining village of Orbiston, Lanarkshire, where he had grown up. Given that he had lost his father in the first world war, he had to mature before his time assuming the role of 'man of the house' by going down the pit after leaving school to bring some money in. This clearly induced in him a certain paternalism which, years later, young players came to value and appreciate. He had grown up in a working class environment where family and kin were important. Busby's experience in football had taught him that the 'soul' or character of a football club was not something that could be left to mere chance like that of a family:

> *"A football club had to have values, human values, a sense of fairness, decency and justice."* (DUNPHY 1991)

This was much more profound than the routine 'rallying call' just before kick off on match day that had been his experience. Busby had participated in the General Strike of 1926 which had lasted just nine days. It had a deep and lasting impression on him and taught him a lesson about:

"Trust and loyalty, about rhetoric and promise, about family and community, most profoundly about power and powerlessness."

It was also to give the young Busby a lesson in unity and dedication to a cause, and he retained socialist values all his life. These were the values he sought to instil in his players at Manchester United beginning with his youth players. This was because young players were much more impressionable than seasoned professionals who thought they 'knew it all'.

Busby's personal life had not been without tragedy. His wife, Jean, had lost four sons who died within a few days of birth. Also his daughter Sheena was born a 'blue baby'. It was only the kindness and knowledge of Manchester City goalkeeper Len Langford's wife, a nurse, that saved her life. It was quite probable that the manager at the time did not even know she was pregnant, such was the remoteness of football managers from the daily lives of the players. These experiences taught him that the events of a player's life affected his performance on the field and he came to the conclusion that a football club had an obligation to care about personal as well as professional life. Busby knew what it was like to be alone, and during a particularly difficult period at Manchester City he decided to pack his suitcase and return to Scotland. Only the intervention of a senior player, Phil McCloy, who cared about young players, persuaded him to stay. Jimmy McMullan, a Scottish international who hailed from Busby's home village of Bellshill, also extended the kind invitation for Busby and his wife to live with them for a while during another difficult period.[18] Football clubs in those days (circa 1928) were cold unfriendly places and according to Dunphy:

This photo of Jimmy Murphy, Tom Curry and Joe Armstrong and their wives typifies the 'family spirit' of United in the 1950s.

> *"Matt was, like other young boys, alone, left to fend for himself in a sport that was savage from top to bottom. Professional soccer was hierarchical; ninety per cent of those at the bottom were crushed, had their spirits broken by cruelty or indifference."*

These experiences had engendered in him a genuine *Humanitas* - a concern for the

plight of other human beings. This led him to "vow that if I ever become a manager I would respect players as individuals who needed individual treatment and thereby try to inspire respect from them."

"They came, we nurtured them, we watched them, we looked after them, they were coached. We were sort of all together type of thing. You became a sort of family - it was a family." INTERVIEW, VIDEO *Official History of Manchester United* (1998)

It was only when Busby was transferred to Liverpool in 1936 that he saw a more humane side of professional football. The manager at Liverpool was George Kay, an extremely caring man who made a deep impression on Matt by the way he ran the club. Whilst senior professionals at other clubs saw young players as mere chattel to abuse both physically and verbally, the Liverpool regime was friendlier - somewhat akin to a family. He vividly remembers the compassionate treatment accorded to an ageing professional called Jimmy McDougall when he became 'surplus to requirements'. Liverpool had the decency to retain him on good wages and retained him again the following year when he did not even play. Furthermore, when he told the club he was retiring a second benefit was paid to him. According to Busby:

"I well remember Liverpool's handling of McDougall. It made a big impression on me, and indeed on all the players because even though it was nothing more than just reward for a loyal servant, there were very few clubs who would have acted similarly in pre-war days." (1957)

When he became manager of Manchester United in 1945 Busby was determined to establish 'a different kind of club', a club that cared for its players whether groundstaff boys or senior internationals. In his autobiography he says that at the start of every season he had an informal chat with all the players and they were told that the staff were there to help them in any way possible. Staff wanted to know if they had any specific problems because brooding about anything would make their football suffer. He wanted to instil in the players, especially the youngsters, a sense of the club as being a home - a place to belong to:

"His aim was to build a team of dedicated youngsters who looked at Manchester

United as their club, something they had grown up with and, therefore, for that reason, almost as much a part of the club, as the bricks and mortar. This was the ideal we had set out to achieve." (MURPHY 1968)

In order to achieve his aim of the club being a homely, friendly place, Busby adopted a 'hands on' approach to every facet of the club's business. He wanted to know everything that affected a player's welfare - his philosophy was, in the words of Dunphy that:

"The club was a family, his family, there would be no secrets, no gaps in communication, no misunderstandings. His office door was always open... not just for football problems, for anything, however, personal and seemingly remote from the game."

Thus Manchester United became Busby's extended family through which he was able, in the words of his son Sandy, to put "his own experience into football". Seeking to correct some of the injustices and maltreatment he had experienced in his personal and professional life this sense of family, of belonging, was symbolised in a way by the club blazer which a player earned only after playing ten first team matches. Those players who had the honour of wearing it felt a sense of satisfaction, pride and achievement - they were now well and truly in the bosom of the family.[19]

SOCIAL LIFE

It would appear that Busby gave his young players a good deal of freedom with regard to their social life away from the club as long as they behaved in a responsible manner. Social life in Manchester during the fifties was vibrant and it is known that the players frequented such clubs as the Plaza, Continental and Cromford. The Cromford was considered to be the most popular club at the time (circa 1954) and was a popular meeting place for sportsmen especially boxers and footballers. These clubs played all the popular music of the day, the rock'n'roll of Elvis Presley and Bill Haley. According to the celebrated disc jockey Jimmy Savile, the Plaza was the social centre of Lancashire and the young Manchester United players went there mainly on Tuesdays and Sundays.[20]

Savile remembers the players as being always well behaved: "Those Manchester

MATT BUSBY'S EXPERIENCES AS A PLAYER FOR MANCHESTER CITY AND LATER LIVERPOOL (ABOVE) HAD A GREAT IMPACT ON HIS POLICIES AS A MANAGER, IN PARTICULAR RELATING TO THE CARE OF HIS PLAYERS AND THEIR FAMILIES.

LIAM WHELAN, WILF MCGUINNESS, TOMMY TAYLOR, BOBBY CHARLTON AND DAVID PEGG BLOW AWAY THE COBWEBS DURING A TYPICAL CLUB OUTING.

United players who came to the Plaza were all model lads. We never had anything remotely resembling trouble." (ROBERTS 1975).

Another popular activity was going to the cinema and Duncan Edwards' mother remembers him going as often as three times a week. The players could use their 'player passes' to get into the cinema for free at certain times of the day. It seems that Busby had brokered an agreement with the managers of certain cinemas so the players could all go together which they often did. Marion Bent, whose husband Geoff died at Munich, remembers the players always doing things together of them being 'one unit'. They all enjoyed having a good time at clubs and the cinema, but they never lost their self control and discipline.

This comaradarie and team spirit is remembered fondly by Wilf McGuinness who has said that the reason he loved the club so much was their growing up together: "we took our first pints together in night clubs, the first time we stayed in hotels abroad we were together, the first time we won trophies was together, we were growing up together". Dennis Viollet has described the relationship between the players as: "more like brothers than pals" and so the family atmosphere Busby was seeking to create at the club was becoming a reality. The players' social and professional lives, however, were disrupted because they had to do National Service and they had to have passes to play for their clubs. For example, Eddie Colman did his National Service with the Royal Corps of Signals at Catterick. This disruption to their professional lives must have had an impact on their football.[21]

Busby did not have an overbearing approach to discipline at the club, believing that the players behaved well through habit (1973). Wilf McGuinness believed that the club knew exactly what was going on socially and any breach of discipline was dealt with by 'a quiet word' rather than a fine. However, the players made sure he did not find out again. Discipline had a positive effect, guiding the players in the right direction. The players actually received a rule book entitled *Training Rules and Instructions* which contained sixteen rules in total. Laurie Cassidy's rule book between 1950-1956, which the author has handled in the Manchester United Museum, shows that the basic rules of the club remained unchanged throughout the period. The main rules were related to smoking (Rule 11) and drinking (Rule 13). Rule eleven is interesting because it states that:

"Smoking is strictly prohibited during training hours, and players are earnestly requested to reduce smoking to the absolute minimum on the day of a match."

Clearly, smoking was something which was tolerated if not actually approved of, even on the day of a match. Perhaps the harmful effects of smoking in relation to athletic activity was not so well known in this period. What is clear, however, is that the club rules were quite reasonable and no excessive constraints were placed on the players by the club. Busby's philosophy seems to have been that self discipline driven by respect for other members of the team and club was more important than rigid rules and regulations. It was his great achievement to bring together young boys from all over the United Kingdom and Ireland and instill in them a spirit of discipline, and co-operation in a highly competitive sport.

It would be rewarding to examine the interaction of Manchester United's youth players in the light of Elias and Dunning's configurational Sociology which was outlined in Chapter One. Issues of tension and tension control in social groups such as football teams were analysed in order to see how the competition for a place on the team, which created tension within groups, could be tempered thus maintaining harmony within the Group. Elias and Dunning refer to this tension as: "the polarity between cooperation and competition within each team". It could be argued that Busby's attempt to create a caring family atmosphere in which a spirit of co-operation rather than conflict existed at the club helped alleviate some of this tension.

We have seen in this chapter that youth development at Manchester United in the fifties was quite a complex process. Schoolboys were brought to the club, placed in lodgings, and found jobs by the club. They then tried to graduate through the various junior teams which was very demanding, and some of them became first team regulars. Contractual arrangements were discussed as well as the players' social lives. The concept that Matt Busby was trying to build a family atmosphere among the young players was analysed in relation to Elias and Dunning's configurational sociology. The next chapter will examine what happened at the training ground. What kind of coaching and training did the young players receive during the period of this study?

NOTES

[1] The youngest player to actually play for Manchester United in a competitive match was probably Jeff Whitefoot who made his League debut at just sixteen years of age (Dykes 1994, p399).

[2] The reserve team.

[3] See also the FA advanced coaching licence EUFA 'A' coaching award, study pack five (1996).

[4] By 'Lower Age' Frank Hannah is referring to junior football.

[5] All four players had significant careers. Pegg died in the Munich disaster (1958).

[6] The players who came through the youth system were: Byrne, Blanchflower, Colman, Doherty, Edwards, Foulkes, Jones, Pegg, Viollet and Whelan.

[7] This includes exercise physiology, bio-mechanics, coaching methodology and psychology.

[8] That is, a City Council bus.

[9] Burnage is a suburb of Manchester lying three miles south of the City Centre.

[10] Bert Fishburn was the team manager.

[11] The FA Premier League rules, section M, youth development, p6.

[12] The apprentice professional scheme was introduced in the early sixties which enabled clubs to sign boys and pay them a salary. If they graduated through this scheme they could sign professional at seventeen. The author progressed through this scheme with Manchester United, signing full professional forms in December 1969.

[13] Stretford Grammar School was less than a fifteen minute walk from Old Trafford. It remains an extremely vibrant educational establishment.

[14] Old Trafford was severely bombed during the war and had to be rebuilt.

[15] By "it gave you nothing" Albert means that players on the groundstaff did not have any special status among their peers. Bill Inglis was a member of the club staff.

[16] Roberts (1975) contains a photograph of players having tea at Mrs Watson's circa 1954. The players photographed are: Charlton, Blanchflower, Edwards, Jones and Taylor.

[17] Olive played two league matches for the club in 1953. He was appointed Assistant Secretary in 1955 before taking over as Secretary following Walter Crickmer's death at Munich in 1958. He retired thirty years later afer giving forty years' loyal service. In 1988 he a club director. (Dykes 1994, p288).

[18] Busby signed for Manchester City in 1928 when just eighteen years of age, and went to live in 'digs' in Manchester (Dunphy 1991, p27).

[19] The club blazer is no longer earned in this way but is acquired by simply signing scholastic forms at the academy.

[20] Now of course Sir Jimmy Savile.

[21] This would make a fascinating study because it involved so many seasoned international players.

**CHAPTER FOUR:
COACHING AND
TRAINING**

MATT BUSBY AND JIMMY MURPHY
PIONEERED A NEW TECHNIQUE THAT
BECAME KNOWN AS 'TRACKSUIT
MANAGEMENT' DEFINED NOT SO MUCH
BY THE CLOTHES THAT THEY WORE
BUT BY THE ATTENTION TO DETAIL
AND 'HANDS-ON' COACHING THEY
SPECIALISED IN.

This chapter develops the themes discussed in Chapter Three and seeks to evaluate the coaching and training of the youth players at Manchester United during the fifties. After exploring, albeit briefly, the origins of coaching in England, it will examine the day-to-day training routine at the club and critically assess the various coaching methods that were used: technical, tactical, physical, psychological and so on. The chapter will also consider to what extent Matt Busby and Jimmy Murphy were coaches in the technical sense of the word in their application of football coaching theory. There will also be a discussion about the aesthetic dimension of football and the extent that the youth players at Manchester United were encouraged to be creative and instinctive in their play and not overly constrained by tactical regimentation. Huizinga's (1970) theory of play is important here, as well as Keller's (Whiting and Masterson 1984) aesthetic concept of mastery which were discussed in Chapter One. Another theme the chapter explores is the revolutionary ideas about how the game should be played emanating from the continent (particularly Central Europe) during the period of our study.

HUNGARY'S 6 - 3 WIN at Wembley in November 1953 was a profound demonstration of a 'new way' of playing the game which had never been seen before in this country. This involved a high level of team play, but also the beauty of individual expression (aesthetics). The chapter will examine the impact these ideas had on coaching at the club vis-a-vis these innovations.

Finally, the vital role of the coaching staff will be discussed in detail including the major question of how Matt Busby's 'philosophy of football' was transmitted to the players via the coaching staff, especially Jimmy Murphy. During extensive field work, the author has been privileged to draw on the important oral testimony of two distinguished former United players: Bill Foulkes and Wilf McGuinness. They both spoke extensively about the coaching and training methods at the club during the fifties for the first time in an academic context. (see Introduction)

WALTER WINTERBOTTOM WROTE ENGLISH FOOTBALL'S FIRST COACHING TEXTBOOK IN 1952, A YEAR BEFORE THE MAGNIFICENT MAGYARS' SUPERB WEMBLEY EXHIBITION. WINTERBOTTOM WAS THE ENGLAND MANAGER AT THE TIME.

THE HISTORY OF COACHING

The late Sir Walter Winterbottom, a former Manchester United player who went on to become the Football Association's Director of Coaching and England team manager from 1946-1962, recalls the coaching and training at the club during his time there circa 1936-38.[1] The club had an extremely simple regime which had been handed down over the years:

> *"You had to walk round the pitch six times and then you had to run round the pitch six times and that was your stamina training, and then a few physical jerks and a little ball practice. In fact the use of the ball for training during the week, apart from the game itself, was very limited... there was no tactical awareness, you just played football, and people didn't have much knowledge of how to help each other, how to build a system."* (TAYLOR AND WARD, 1975)

Winterbottom states that there was a great deal of secrecy prevailing in the game regarding the transmission of information, a reluctance to discuss football issues with other people in the game, even one's own team mates. He cites the example of one player who, having passed on some technical advice urged him to "keep it to yourself". Former England international George Hardwick asserts that football knowledge was disseminated orally during the forties and the written word was frowned on and not generally accepted within the game. This was because football had existed for such a long time without any theory being applied to it. When coaching manuals finally appeared Hardwick claims that many people did not like it because such knowledge "had never been put in a book of words".[2]

The general attitude towards coaching during the pre-war period was that it was not necessary. Stanley Matthews, the celebrated England International, states that even technical ball work was discouraged in training because it was felt that: "if you have too much ball, you're gonna be tired of it on the Saturday".[3] Nat Lofthouse, the former Bolton Wanderers and England international endearingly known as the 'Lion of Vienna' following his brave display against Austria in 1952, states that "years ago, the ball never played a part as far as training was concerned. It was just lapping round the ground for about half to three-quarters of an hour." This summarises the attitude to formal coaching and training at the beginning of the fifties - nothing had changed for decades.

Walter Winterbottom, in his coaching book (1952), asserts that the FA first became interested in formalised coaching in 1934, but it was not until his appointment as Director of Coaching in 1946 that coaching in this country began to be taken seriously. Winterbottom felt that playing standards in England needed to improve and this could only be achieved through coaching. He says the following about why coaching is important:

> *"The lack of knowledge was abysmal really within the game, and the idea of coaching was to bring along players with more knowledge of how to keep fit, how to train, how to use tactics, the various skills, the variation of skill ... we were so insular that we wouldn't believe other methods could be used for doing things, that other ways of playing the game could be better than ours, that had to change, of course."*

Winterbottom had the vision to introduce coaching courses for aspiring coaches through a comprehensive coaching scheme which certified coaches at a variety of levels. Furthermore, a series of instructional textbooks were introduced by the FA beginning with Winterbottom's 1952 manual. This has been followed over the years by Wade (1967) and Hughes (1973, 1980 and 1990). An excellent example of the European approach to coaching is Csandi (1965).[4]

This, then, was the coaching background in England in which Matt Busby began to instruct his young charges at Manchester United at the beginning of the fifties.

YOUTH COACHING AND TRAINING AT MANCHESTER UNITED

Miller (1994) has claimed that Matt Busby was the focal point of almost every important development in the game and this was especially true with regard to his approach to the coaching and training of youth players at Manchester United. We saw in Chapter One how he and Major Buckley at Wolverhampton Wanderers were the pioneers in the sphere of recruiting players to their respective clubs. An important aspect of youth development is the quality of coaching they receive once they arrive at the club. Busby's leadership in this regard was peerless and fully justifies the epithet 'Bryn boru' (leader of men) that his grandfather used to describe his influence on the streets near his home as a boy. Little

JIMMY MURPHY'S ENTHUSIASM FOR FOOTBALL SAW HIM GET THE BEST OUT OF STARS SUCH AS DUNCAN EDWARDS (LEFT), DENNIS VIOLLET (BACK TO CAMERA) AND LIAM WHELAN (RIGHT). HIS COMMITMENT TO BUSBY'S SYTEM WAS TOTAL.

THE FACILITIES IN THE OLD TRAFFORD GYM HAVE BEEN DESCRIBED AS BASIC, SO AN EXERCISE BIKE LIKE THE ONE PICTURED CAUSED QUITE A STIR.

did his grandfather know just how prophetic that nickname would be (Glanville, 1994).

Busby's philosophy of football was formed during his schooldays in Bellshill. His three heroes as a boy were Alex James, Hughie Gallagher and Jimmy McMullan who all hailed from Bellshill.[5] They were the sons of Scottish Football and idolised by the nation because of their exploits when Scotland famously defeated England 5-1 at Wembley in 1928. They became known as the 'Wembley Wizards' and were arguably the greatest Scottish team of all time. Busby particularly liked James. He loved the way he played the game: his trickery, invention, charisma, flair and arrogance on the field. Busby's football life was inspired by players of James's ilk: Puskas, di Stefano, Charlton, Law and Best. Although the young Busby had never been acquainted with great poetry or listened to the music of Beethoven or Mozart, seeing the Wembley Wizards perform on the field enchanted him. He saw beauty in their play, understood what it was and delighted in wonders of the imagination. He knew that through football he could express himself - football was the medium by which he could find genuine fulfilment. (Dunphy 1991).

Cliff Lloyd, a former colleague at Liverpool, has said that a football team is a reflection of its manager's philosophy: "Matt was a purist. He loved his players to express themselves." Manchester United's youth policy during the fifties can thus be seen as a reflection of Busby's approach to the game. His inherent belief that football should be played in a certain way - it was an art that could enthral both players and spectators. He attempted to put his philosophy of football into practice at Manchester United, starting with the young players who could be more easily influenced by his ideas.

Busby believed that the foundation of a football club lay on the training ground, Saturday's match was a reflection of what took place in training. This was where character was nurtured and developed, skills honed and refined. His basic coaching philosophy was to influence the character of the gifted young player and to teach the basic lessons of what it meant to be a professional footballer. The coaching staff should not have to teach them how to play, that is, they did not need a great deal of technical coaching as they should have the basic ability when they arrive if the scouts had done their jobs properly. All that was required was for the schoolboy bad habits to be broken just like a horse, and be properly moulded and assimilated into 'the family' which was Manchester United. They must be willing to learn the simple lesson of developing good character: honesty, determination, integrity, dedication and loyalty. These qualities were, for Busby, just as

THE FAMILY SPIRIT FOSTERED BY MATT BUSBY IS EVIDENT HERE:
ABOVE: THE BUSBY BABES AT THE HEIGHT OF THEIR FAME; (LEFT TO RIGHT) JOHNNY BERRY; DUNCAN EDWARDS; MARK JONES; ROGER BYRNE AND DENNIS VIOLLET.

important as football ability. With young boys like these he could grow 'good apples'.

Busby believed that good coaching was important but he was ever wary of the dangers of over coaching: "the great danger of coaching is that it might take the fun out of football". Coaching for Busby was a simple process according to former player Henry Cockburn:

> *"Matt always used to say 'keep the ball flowing'. When I finished playing and went on coaching courses they had invented one touch and two touch games as part of the coaching system, it was only then I realised Matt had us playing like that unknowingly."* [6]
> (DUNPHY 1991)

What Cockburn is saying here is that Busby was not a coach in the formal or technical sense of the word, but rather a preacher of a simple gospel. Football was a simple game, only made complex or difficult by bad players and poor coaches. The late Charlie Mitten, another former player, concurs with this view, stating that Busby and Murphy were not coaches in a theoretical way, but that both men understood players and knew how to motivate them.[7] Eamon Dunphy saw Busby and Murphy as teachers whose great strength was not the over-use of football jargon, but rather the teaching of the simple realities of the professional game, the basic principles of team play. This would help a player to grow to maturity. Both men from the outset "preached the Gospel of movement and skill allied to simplicity".

One of the major questions this book is seeking to answer is what the actual coaching and training was like for youth players at Manchester United on a daily basis during the fifties? How were Busby's ideas put into practice? You will remember from the previous chapter that the youth players were only able to train at night because of work or college commitments during the day. Therefore, the main training and coaching of youth players took place at the Cliff Training Ground, Salford, on a Tuesday and Thursday evening.[8] These were extremely important sessions in which a good deal of vital instruction took place. The coaching was extremely dynamic led by Jimmy Murphy, Busby's assistant manager who was also responsible for the coaching of youth. He was assisted by Bert Whalley who was to die at Munich in 1958. Bill Foulkes offers the following insight on the coaching at the club in 1950 when he first arrived as an amateur player. He used to travel by train to the club after working down the pit all day in St Helens:

"I used to warm up myself, I used to do a lot of running because I got very little ball work during the week. The only chance I'd got of doing ball work was on Tuesday and Thursday. The rest of the week I used to run. As soon as I came here it was all ball: we just played with a ball, worked it all the time. Jimmy Murphy and Bert Whalley - it was all ball. Passing practices, movement, shadow play which was really imagination. We didn't do anything in theory at all. On the pitch it was all working and we were just so happy to be there, a privilege for us to be there and we just enjoyed it... Jimmy and Bert would be giving instructions, giving advice.

"It was not planned, not particularly planned, just using the ball, playing the ball. And then after a while we'd do certain practices like technique practices for heading. Heading, control, passing, particularly passing. Jim was a stickler for passing. Accuracy of passing, weight of passing, and he was always stating this you know. But then after that it would be a short sided game, and then we'd have a full scale pitch match. And that was basically what we did Tuesday and Thursday - that's what we did." INTERVIEW

At first glance what Foulkes describes seems quite basic but on closer examination it is clear that work with the ball was deemed to be very important, this was to improve technique, as well as work 'off the ball' described as movement. It is notable that Foulkes mentions that the coaches did 'shadow play' with them in training. Shadow play is quite a complex coaching technique to help acquire a higher level of team work and game understanding. It involves practising soccer movements with the ball but with restricted or even no opposition. This required the players to use their imagination in order to rehearse specific movement patterns in the game. Shadow play is quite a formal coaching technique and its use by Murphy and Whalley dispels the long pervading myth that United players did everything by instinct or intuition. Murphy placed great emphasis on the ability to pass the ball properly with the correct accuracy and weight. There was clearly a lot of intensive coaching going on. However, the emphasis was on the practical application of skill rather than theoretical posturing.

Wilf McGuinness, who arrived at the club in 1953, three years after Foulkes, describes training on Tuesday and Thursday as follows:

"Jimmy Murphy and Bert Whalley were the coaches. Jimmy was assistant manager as well and he'd be down there and he would, during the game or before the game, tell us something of what he wanted individually and collectively as a group. Then once the game started he would stop the game and point out certain things and stand on the side. He didn't stop it all the time you know he let it flow. But if there was something very important he would emphasise he'd intervene. So that's how the form of coaching, the training worked - we didn't just go into a game - we did what would be termed 'loosening up' now. But to us it was about four laps say of the pitch and ten sides. You know it was running, you had to run and then various exercises depending on the weather of course ... we arrived before six and finished at eight so it was like a couple of hours." INTERVIEW

McGuinness says that training lasted two hours and that Murphy did a lot of coaching during a game, stopping it from time to time to make a point. This is called 'freezing the play' in modern coaching parlance. This once again demonstrates the fact that Murphy's approach to coaching was ahead of its time. There also seems to have been little emphasis on physical training.

We can conclude from the evidence of Foulkes and McGuinness that training on Tuesday and Thursday evening consisted of an element of physical, technical and tactical aspects within a two hour timeframe. The main emphasis, however, was on technical and tactical work rather than physical fitness. It was assumed that actually playing this game in training would keep the players fit.

FOOTBALL AND AESTHETICS

We have seen that Busby was sensitive to the artistic qualities of football, and in a speech he gave on receiving the Freedom of Manchester in November 1967 he said the following:

> *"There are two aspects of the game that have always impressed me. I love its drama, its smooth playing skill and its great occasions, for example the Cup Final in the great arena at Wembley. I feel a sense of romance, wonder, and mystery, a sense of poetry."* (Miller 1994)

Jimmy Murphy (1968) who hailed from the Rhondda Valley has also said the following:

> *"In my teens I played the organ in Treorchy Parish Church and I still find Beethoven, Lizst and Chopin played on the piano a great source of relief and inspiration from the tensions of big time football."*

It is clear that both men loved the artistry, beauty and aesthetic qualities that football at its best could evoke. However, they were also conscious of the fact that beautiful flowing football was not always winning football. They understood that to be successful in professional football management a balance had to be found between artistry and other qualities such as fitness, determination and courage. Their aim was to instill these qualities in the youth players at Manchester United through the coaching and training programme. The responsibility for this was delegated to Murphy when he first joined the club in 1945. Wilf McGuinness has said that the football the young players produced was not all improvised:

> *"In my opinion it was an idea that you just went out and played and do what you want - it didn't happen. I didn't find it that way at all. Bobby Charlton was coached, I was coached, Duncan Edwards, who was the greatest, was coached you know in areas to play and how to play, but it was coached in an understanding way. We did shadow play ... playing against nobody sometimes playing without a ball, well playing with the ball most of the time. Going up and down the field, how we would*

get it. For instance if the fullback gets it, if his winger's free give it the winger. If the winger can't go anywhere he'll play it to the inside forwards or wing half so if it's given back to you obviously he can't go forward so you change the play. So the left half comes looking for it - and when he gets it he feeds his winger cause it's their job to feed the forwards. While they're feeding the forwards the centre forward is going on runs and while he's going on runs the defence is on the swivel and that's the time when you catch them square - you can play the through ball and this was taught to us ... this was Jimmy's technique and it was 'no! no! no! no!' if things went wrong 'no! no! no! no! I want this and I want that', and he even told Bobby Charlton. His encouragement to Bobby was 'it doesn't matter where you are if you're in a shooting position think of shooting - finalise the move either with a shot or header'. So Bobby got it in his mind, 'I'm thinking of shooting'."

This is a splendid example of organised, systematic coaching in order to achieve a high level of team work. The players are given ideas, and a pattern of play in which these ideas can be expressed within this overall pattern of play. I then asked Wilf to what extent the players were allowed to express their individuality by playing artistic, creative football: He said the following:

"If it was his own way and it was successful that's all right, it's when you're not successful that it needs to be knocked on the head... In the end it was your natural ability. It wasn't a coach for what the coach believed in solely, it was for a pattern of play. He gave us ideas on how to play to a pattern where everyone would get a feel of the ball. Now, if it was right to go forward, even like now, feed your forwards as quickly as possible - we were always taught that. If you can't do that you've got to use your imagination or do something else or change the play. But they didn't want you to take chances as well. I can remember trying to do a trick like running toward my own goal and backheeling it. Well it went to one of the opposition and he went clean through and nearly scored. He didn't score, but even Matt Busby told me never to try that trick again. But I wasn't a tricky player. He never would, like Jimmy Murphy, like you throwing the ball square in your own half just in case you got put out of the game." INTERVIEW

What McGuinness is saying is that players were allowed to improvise (use their imagination) but only after they had taken into account the safety and risk factors of the situation they were in on the field. It was no use to the team if a player was trying to do tricks and this resulted in a goal being conceded. The 'backheel' is an excellent example of this, and McGuinness is scolded by Busby for attempting to be clever. Therefore, the players were encouraged to use their imagination on the field, but be wary of taking risks in dangerous areas. Creative instinct must to some degree conform to the demands of team play.

When examining this, one is reminded of the theories of Huizinga and Keller which were discussed in Chapter One. Huizinga, you will remember, asserted that the increased organisation and competitive nature of sport had resulted in a loss or reduction in the play or fun aspects playing sport engendered. Huizinga argues that sport had moved from the sphere of play to being just *a thing sue generis*. The golfer Arnold Palmer has claimed that to be successful in sport an element of fun must be retained:

> *"Palmer claimed that in the final days of preparation for a big competition he must have complete freedom from care; that he must be free to play a round or not, and even abandon a round if he felt a lack of enthusiasm for it."* (MCINTOSH 1963)

In other words, for Palmer nothing was more important than the natural urge to play even when competing at the highest level of sport. Indeed, to be successful something of the natural play element must be retained.

Busby and Murphy applied Huizinga's theory unwittingly with their famous dictum to the players before they went out: "go out and enjoy yourselves". Hans Keller's theory of mastery within aesthetics can also be applied to Busby's philosophy of football (see Chapter Two). Keller argues that mastery itself is demonstrable - it is something which can be taught, presumably by a teacher or coach. Since mastery can be taught it must conform to generally accepted rules laid down by the prevailing culture. Keller argues that adherence to mastery can be harmful because it can restrict the complete development of natural talent. In other words to become a 'master' one can lose an important aspect of creative instinct. One does not explore the possibilities but rather continues to practise 'safe mastery'. However, it is the creative genius who breaks all the established rules of mastery creating new rules and then breaking them again. This is the truly creative artist.

BILL FOULKES: UNITED'S LONGEST-SERVING PLAYER JOINED UNITED STRAIGHT FROM THE ST HELENS PIT.

Thus for Keller, success and creativity in sport can be inter-related.

Busby himself was celebrated as a manager who recognised the need for mastery but also the need for individual genius. This can be seen by the great players his youth policy produced in the fifties: Charlton, Colman, Edwards and Viollet being excellent examples. It was his genius that he recognised that it was sometimes necessary to reject the rules of mastery (theoretical coaching) in order to allow individual brilliance to flourish. Keller cites an example of this when Manchester United played Portuguese champions Benfica in the European Cup in 1966. Busby's masterly instructions were to play a defensive game and George Best (a superbly creative player) was asked not to play his natural creative, instinctive game but rather adopt a role within a sound tactically defensive team pattern. This was vital because the team were trying to protect a one goal lead from the first leg in Manchester. Thus a masterly strategy should be adopted - no-risk football should be played. What actually happened astounded the football world making George Best an international star. Best contravened Busby's instructions and scored two impertinent goals within the first ten minutes of the match. United went on to win 5 - 1. This is a superb example of the tension between mastery and genius when applied to football. It is also a supreme example of Busby's ability to restrain his own concept of mastery when he realised he had something to learn which might lead to something entirely original. Indeed it can be argued that this was the very core of his success as a Manager for more than twenty years.

It is worth comparing Keller's concept of mastery with that of the music of The Beatles, the rock group of the sixties. Barry Miles (1997) has argued that because John Lennon and Paul McCartney (the group's principal songwriters) had no theoretical musical knowledge, they did not know when they were breaking the formal rules, or even when they were doing something original. Aeolian cadences became part of the Beatle legend and were frequently mentioned in the popular press.[9] However, John Lennon has said:

"To this day I don't have any idea what they are, they sound like exotic birds."

And in reference to his famous song *Yesterday*, Paul McCartney has said the following:

"I woke up with a lovely tune in my head. I thought, that's great, I wonder what that is?... I got out of bed, sat at the piano, found G, found F sharp minor 7th - that

leads you through then to B and E minor, and finally back to E. It all leads forward logically. I liked the melody a lot but because I'd dreamed it I couldn't believe I'd written it. I thought, no, I've never written like this before. But I had the tune, which was the most magic thing. And you have to ask yourself, where did it come from? But you don't ask yourself too much or it might go away."

McCartney, by experimentation, found out little tricks as he went along. He considered taking a formal course in music theory but decided that:

"Music is such a beautiful innocent thing for me, a magic thing, that I don't want it ever to smack of homework, that would ruin it all."

This equates (musically) with Busby and Keller's idea of self-expression and improvisation: artists should not be bound by rules or theoretical concepts. The true artist would have to break some rules. Alex Ferguson, United's current manager, concurs with this view. Having witnessed Ryan Giggs scoring a goal of breathtaking brilliance in a cup semi-final replay against Arsenal in April 1999, he said the following:

"The part of Ryan Giggs that made that goal is something I could never have put into him... it is uncoachable. What we saw was the ultimate expression of the natural gifts he has always had since the day he came to us as a 13 year old."
(SUNDAY TIMES, 18TH APRIL 1999)

Ferguson's comment about Ryan Giggs' flair and individualism is an eloquent expression of Huizinga and Keller's theories.

RYAN GIGGS CELEBRATES HIS BRILLIANT GOAL AGAINST ARSENAL IN 1999. MORE REGIMENTED COACHING WOULD SURELY HAVE DENIED US THIS MEMORABLE MOMENT.

EUROPEAN INFLUENCES (HUNGARY)

In November 1953 Hungary famously defeated England 6 - 3 at Wembley Stadium in London. It was England's first defeat by foreign opposition on home soil and the result sent shock waves around the football world. The Hungarians introduced to this country revolutionary concepts in the sphere of tactics and team work and provided the foundation for the concept of 'total football' which the Dutch re-introduced two decades later at the 1974 World Cup.[10] We saw above that they produced a method and style of playing football which had never been seen on these shores before. They had, in the words of Dr Rogan Taylor, virtually "reinvented football" (The Guardian, 27th April 1999). This involved subtle interchanging of position, quick incisive passing and a higher level of technical and tactical expertise. In short this was a much more 'intellectual' form of football. A major innovation was the introduction of a 'deep-lying' centre-forward (Hidekuti) who played much deeper than the traditional British model, making it much more difficult for him to be marked by the opposition. This caused a great deal of tactical confusion among defenders. Hidekuti was also much more technically and tactically proficient. The Hungarian performance at Wembley that day led future England manager Ron Greenwood, to say the following:

> *"I was watching a team playing the way I felt football should be played, and to me it was a revelation and it made a great impression on me. I felt there and then that if I ever became in charge of a team, that's near enough the way I'd want to play. At that time we were playing a lot of football in this country where it was the long ball up to the big centre-forward and knock back and what have you and Hungary's passing angles were unbelievable. They would bring so many people into the play by knocking it up, getting it back, knocking it wide and moving again, and the movement was complete. In other words the man on the ball had about three alternatives. Consequently, the angles and the movement caused catastrophic disaster in the English defence. They were chasing shadows half the time."*
> (TAYLOR AND WARD 1975)

Willy Meisl (1955), an Austrian observer, said that the Hungarian display had exposed the fact that British soccer had been in decline because individuality, inventiveness, and experimentation had been frowned on and the adventurous spirit in players suppressed.

> *"The so-called speed by which the Hungarians defeated the Englishmen and made them look so ridiculous for long periods was not one of legs, but originated in the cerebral part of their anatomy. Players of perfect technique and in full possession of their individualities, their fancy and fantasy bridled but not extinguished, beat our fast, well conditioned, but unimaginative 'robots'."*

On reading Meisl's comments one is reminded of the aesthetic qualities that Huizinga and Keller enthused about in the previous section. Clearly the Hungarians believed in playing beautiful football! Meisl believed strongly that English football's overly defensive style of play, the 'safety first' attitude among coaches and managers, had been exposed by the Hungarians to be a 'false god'. He concluded that, "good football cannot thrive, cannot even begin to flourish without imagination". There was a collision of styles: guile and craft as opposed to speed and strength. In summary: brain beat brawn, this was the fundamental lesson the Hungarians taught us. Furthermore, England's long standing opposition to coaching had led to disaster.

Meisl believed that the way forward for English football was to free young players from the shackles of playing to order. In other words they must be allowed to be more creative, inventive and original in their thinking. In order to do this young players had to be trained and coached properly. This is precisely what Busby was attempting to do with his youth policy at Manchester United.

What impact did these new ideas from Europe have on the young players at United? Bill Foulkes had the following observation:

> *"They'd so many short passes which we hadn't seen before. Possession play which we hadn't seen before and from them we learned that there was a pace to the game, they could change the pace of the game... They could slow the game down, keep possession of the ball and then they*

HUGO MEISL: INVENTOR OF THE FIRST PROFESSIONAL LEAGUE IN MAINLAND EUROPE (AUSTRIA) AND THE MITROPA CUP, FORERUNNER OF THE EUROPEAN CHAMPIONS' CUP, MEISL'S OPINIONS ABOUT THE DECLINE OF ENGLISH FOOTBALL RANG TRUE IN 1953.

could speed it up and this is what they did. I was quite impressed with that. Then it was tactical, the other side was tactical. There were two strikers not one, two out and out strikers you know - Hidekuti. They weren't the big strong type of players that I was used to playing against. They were quick, mobile, skilful players - a different type of player. We had to learn a different way of playing and quickly!" INTERVIEW

Foulkes's comments can be usefully compared with those of Wilf McGuinness:

"Yes, they were talked about - how to play the Hungarian way and all this. We were told 'Watch these players...' they were talked of as the best in the World. This is what we were aiming for, you know. This was discussed, we went, we went, I think it was the year later. They played West Germany at Wembley because I think in 1954, I think West Germany won the World Cup.[11] They played there and we went down as a club and I was only 17, went down for the day on a train to watch that game in an afternoon at Wembley. The club took us down." INTERVIEW

Bill Foulkes was hugely impressed with the Hungarian ability to control the pace of the game, as well as their tactical innovations. He noticed, also, that their forwards were much more mobile than the players he was used to playing against in England. He asserts, tellingly, that the main impact they had was to force them as players to "learn a different way of playing and quickly". They were obviously extremely receptive to these new concepts of playing. The most interesting observation made by McGuinness was the fact that the club (Busby and Murphy) took the entire playing squad to watch the World Champions play Hungary at Wembley. This demonstrates how important Busby and Murphy felt it was to expose the young Manchester United players to European influences. They felt that watching the best players and teams in Europe (and the World) 'live' could only benefit their own as well as their young players' football education.

THE COACHING AND TRAINING STAFF

For any football club to be successful at developing its own players the appointment of a good coaching and training staff is essential. Jimmy Murphy was Busby's first appointment when he was appointed Manager in 1945. Murphy was a former Welsh international and was was given responsibility for the reserve team as well coaching the junior players on Tuesday and Thursday nights. His role will be examined in more detail shortly.

Another key appointment was Bert Whalley (later to die in the Munich disaster). He became Murphy's assistant as Busby explains:

"I put Bert Whalley as Jimmy's Assistant. A soft spoken studious type, a good judge and a particularly good influence on youngsters... my coaching was in good hands." (BUSBY 1957)

Very little is generally known about Bert Whalley's role at the club during the fifties. He had been a former player at the club and played thirty-three times for the first team before an eye injury ended his career. Whalley was also a Methodist lay preacher which lays to rest the long standing myth that United were a 'Catholic club'. When it came to the business of professional football:

"Busby sought to surround himself with decent dependable men no matter what their religious convictions were." (DUNPHY 1991)

It is clear from the testimony of Bill Foulkes and Wilf McGuinness that Whalley was an extremely important man. Foulkes has the following memories of him:

"He was an outstanding man and person... he was a big help to me particularly on Tuesday and Thursday evenings. He would tell me what's going on during the week and whether I was going to be selected for either the reserves or the 'A' team or the first team. He'd sort of fill me in what happened during the week. And he used to write to me. Once a week I'd get a letter telling me what's happened at the club, how the reserves had played, and he did the same when I was in the army doing two years' National Service. I'd get a letter once a week from Bert Whalley telling me what's happened at the club keeping me informed what was

happening so I knew everything that was going on. Handwritten - never missed. And also, if he saw me play in the first team or even in the reserves, he gave a few notes - and in those little notes I learned a hell of a lot."[12] INTERVIEW

What is fascinating about the above comment is the fact that Whalley was so sensitive about Foulkes's welfare that he took it upon himself to write regularly to inform him about events at the club. He even did this when Foulkes was absent from the club doing National Service. This indicates the kind of man he was. McGuinness makes the following comment about Whalley's coaching ability:

"He'd be there Tuesdays and Thursdays as well - he was the main one under Jimmy and he was a real gentleman ... I think Bert he was more a coach - he was a coach, definitely a coach in fact ... a good coach, not a loud coach." INTERVIEW

It seems from the above that not only was Whalley an outstanding coach he, was also extremely concerned about the welfare of his players, as his correspondence with Foulkes demonstrates. This is an example of the non-technical or psychological aspect of coaching - the caring about individual players' welfare that helped to engender a love for the club and the feeling that they were part of a family as discussed in Chapter Three. Wilf McGuinness says that loyalty and team spirit - the sense of family was:

"Passed on not only through training, but it came from the Matt Busby family it you like - the Busby Babes tradition of winning things.[13] *You know when you're winning things and going on tours. All this was the bonding and it just grew ... it was the way we were looked after, the impression we got that here was a family club and that was the feeling we got - that these people are gonna look after us.*

"Matt Busby, we didn't see a lot of him but when we saw him he made us feel good. When I went to other clubs I didn't ever see the manager you know, and I was kept waiting in the corridor with my mam and dad stood there. We [the players] became good pals, we went for lunches together.

"If you grow up together there's a bond there and there's still that bond there. That's

why we've still got the former players [Association] ... we used to go for lunches together, we didn't have our lunch at the club in those days.[14] We used to go to a place called 'Snack Time'... then we'd go out together at night to the cinemas and dance halls - we were pals. We went to each other's houses and digs and then went on holiday to Ashington with Bobby Charlton. Who wants to go to Ashington! Eddie Colman and myself went up there with Bobby for a week's holiday. And then we all went over to Butlin's together, [it was] part of growing up." INTERVIEW

Once again we see McGuinness picking up the theme of Manchester United being a 'family club'. The young players did things together. Staff at the club, including Whalley, thought that good coaching was important, but equally important was looking after the boys' welfare, instilling in them family values such as loyalty and respect for one another. This was important both on and off the field. Bert Whalley's approach to the handling of young players is a supreme example of this philosophy.

Another important member of staff was Arthur Powell. He did no actual coaching but had a vital job as youth trainer as well as "overseeing the domestic duties of the groundstaff". Bill Foulkes offers the following portrait of him:

"Arthur Powell was basically in charge of collecting the kit on match days, making sure that it was taken to the laundry and cleaned. Making sure that all the kit was laid out - basically he was sort of an 'odd job' man around the place really. Very reliable, good personality and everybody loved him. He didn't do any coaching at all."

Wilf McGuinness remembers Arthur as:

"A nice man. His duties weren't really football. He'd be what you'd call the kit man now, a helper. He had a First Aid St John's as well you know, he knew how to first aid. He was a nice man and he was the one who had to tell you that you had to go to bed in Switzerland and things like that and sometimes you'd say 'give over Arthur'."[15]

Characters like Arthur Powell are very important in a football club - keeping dressing room spirits high, and lifting the players when they were feeling low. He embodied the

esprit de corps - the spirit of community at Manchester United.

Bill Inglis had a similar role to that of Arthur Powell. He had been a former player having first joined the club in 1925 then leaving to play for Sheffield Wednesday and Northampton Town. He rejoined the club in 1934 as assistant trainer. He retired in 1961 and was succeeded by Wilf McGuinness who had retired because of serious injury. Bill Foulkes has the following memory of him:

> *"And then we had Bill Inglis who was again a former player who did the job in the reserves. He was like the reserve team trainer. No he wasn't a coach, he was like a father figure. He'd give us a few quiet little words here and there on match days."*

Foulkes description of Inglis as being a 'father figure' picks up once again the recurring theme of family and care.

Although he worked primarily with the first team players it would be remiss if Tom Curry's name was not mentioned. He was appointed to the staff in 1934. A native of South Shields, he played for Newcastle United and Stockport County. Curry worked for both the England national team (1938) and the British Olympic team (1948) before joining United from Carlisle as first team trainer. Curry was a great believer in physical fitness and also supervised the players' remedial massage. Wilf McGuinness says that Curry often attended the youth training sessions on Tuesday and Thursday nights to offer assistance, where it was needed. This demonstrates, yet again, the importance the senior staff attached to the youth policy.

We shall now look in detail at the role of Jimmy Murphy, Busby's Assistant Manager. Busby had first played against Murphy before the war when Murphy was playing for West Bromich Albion and Busby was at Manchester City. They met again during the war in Bari, Italy, when Busby was managing an army eleven and Murphy was in charge of a service sports recreation centre for troops who had defeated Rommel's Africa Korps in the Western Desert. Murphy was conducting a coaching session and Busby was a casual observer. He saw immediately the qualities he was looking for in an assistant having accepted an offer to manage Manchester United:

> *"It was his attitude, his command, his enthusiasm and his whole driving, determined action and word power that caused me to say to myself, 'he's the man for me'. He was*

the man I needed to help in my overall plan for Manchester United... He was the man who would help me create a pattern that would run through the several teams of players from fifteen years of age upwards to the first team." (BUSBY 1973)

We have seen that Murphy was given the responsibility of coaching the reserves and junior teams at the club, and he worked at this with an energy and passion that would have destroyed a less capable man. He never drove a car and travelled to work each day by taxi or train - working seventy or eighty hours a week was not uncommon for him.

McGuinness offers the following glimpse of Murphy's work as a coach:

"Well he was the main coach of all levels except Matt Busby. He wouldn't interfere with the first team unless, well it was one of his boys like Duncan Edwards, Eddie Colman and Bobby Charlton he could talk to in private... He always knew he was the bosses number two, he was brilliant - we never even dreamt of him being anything other than the boss and Jimmy. It was never going to be Jimmy and the boss - never... He'd even take you in a room and talk to you for hours on football – there were a lot of one-to-ones. He left an impression with you, you know, and I would say ninety nine percent of the players who made it would say I wouldn't have made it this high without Jimmy Murphy." INTERVIEW

Indeed Bobby Charlton (1967) has said that Murphy instilled in him the basic art of the game, making the basics of football technique a part of his nature. Murphy never usurped Busby and gladly accepted his role as his assistant. He received many offers to manage clubs in his own right but turned them all down believing that Manchester United was his life's work. However, he was no mere 'yes man' according to Busby, but rather he would always offer his honest opinion during discussions. However, having made his point, he always accepted Busby's decision as final. Busby valued his judgement of players and handling of young boys extremely highly. It is interesting that McGuinness talks about Murphy having 'one-to-one' discussions with the players, this indicates that he understood the importance of giving the young players personal attention in order to forge relations and get to know them better. He was doing this well before sports

JIMMY MURPHY'S POWERS OF MOTIVATION WERE LEGENDARY. HERE HE IS WITH BOBBY CHARLTON AND POST-MUNICH RECRUIT ERNIE TAYLOR, EXHORTING THEM WITH TYPICAL GUSTO.

psychology became popular in the coaching world. When one considers the number of great players the club produced during the fifties McGuinness's statement that ninety-nine percent of them owed their success to him is a tremendous tribute to his work and influence as a coach. The esteem in which Murphy is held at the club, even today, is exemplified by the unveiling of a bust in his memory at the Manchester United Museum in 1999. The ceremony was attended by many of his former players, including Bobby Charlton.

Dunphy (1991) offers the following glimpse of Murphy at work:

> *"Jimmy worked from nine in the morning until late at night; first with the full-time pros until lunchtime, then the afternoons on remedial teaching. At six o'clock on Tuesdays and Thursdays he'd be at the Cliff with the youths, part-time pros and amateurs. There was no going through the motions at nights. These youngsters were the future, Jimmy was as hard on them as the older pros. He liked to get to the pub for a couple of pints of ale before closing time. He smoked like a chimney. It would be eleven thirty when he got home to a silent house, the embers burning on his morning fire... football was his life, from day to day, hour to hour, minute to minute... he would laugh and joke, there was a real warmth about him but whenever the subject changed from football he would switch it back."*

Murphy was dedicated to one cause, and one cause only - the success of Manchester United. As a coach he set very high standards and was extremely hard to please. He would often be out on the training ground until five in the afternoon exhorting the basic elements of the game. Murphy was not a complicated coach. He believed that text book theories were no use in the practical world of football. He taught a simple set of basic principles on which the game had been founded: the importance of passing, changing the point of attack, defending, getting the ball back by working hard as a team. Having talent was not enough - that was taken for granted. Just as important for Murphy were personal qualities such as: desire, determination, courage and loyalty to the club.

It is clear from this evidence that Jimmy Murphy was a tremendous coach in every sense of the meaning of that word. He was well organised, extremely knowledgeable, and very passionate about the game. His contribution to the success of Manchester United's youth policy in the fifties is inestimable.

This chapter has been concerned with the following themes in relation to the coaching and training at Manchester United during the fifties. Firstly, we have analysed the coaching at the club in the fifties in the context of the general attitude towards coaching that prevailed in England: physically, technically and tactically and in the light of two major theories: Huizinga's theory of play and Keller's theory of mastery. Secondly, we have examined the influence of European ideas about coaching to see what impact, if any, they had on Manchester United's youth policy. Finally, we have analysed the contribution of the coaching staff to the success of the youth policy with a particular spotlight on Jimmy Murphy.

The final chapter of this study will take this a stage further where we will be examining the influence of youth competitions in England and Europe on the development of young players at Manchester United during the period of this study.

FOOTNOTES

[1] Winterbottom was a qualified teacher taking a Diploma in Physical Education at Carnegie College after finishing playing (Taylor and Ward 1995).

[2] Hardwick played for Middlesborough and Oldham Athletic. He played for England against the USA in the 1950 World Cup in Brazil, when they were defeated 1 - 0. This was, and remains, one of the greatest upsets in World Cup history.

[3] Stanley Matthews was football's first knight, and also has the distinction of being the first European Footballer of the Year (1956).

[4] The FA Coaching Scheme was reconstructed in 1996 with the introduction of the category 'A' and 'B' coaching licence. These are now validated by the Union of European Football Associations (EUFA). These new courses have replaced the FA Preliminary and Full Coaching Certificate which had formed the core of the FA's Instructional Courses since the fifties.

[5] Jimmy McMullan was later to play with Busby at Manchester City and he lived with the McMullans during a difficult period (Busby 1973, p119-20).

[6] Henry Cockburn was an England international and won a League championship and FA Cup winners medal with Manchester United (1948 and 1952). See Dykes (1994).

[7] Mitten played in the 1948 Cup final with Henry Cockburn. He left the club in 1950 and controversially went to play in Bogata, Columbia, which was outside the jurisdiction of FIFA, the game's Governing Body.

[8] The Cliff Training Ground is still in use as I write. However, the training of most youth players moved to a new complex at Carrington, Greater Manchester in August 2002.

[9] For further discussion of aeolian cadences see Kennedy (1980).

[10] Total soccer refers to a system involving constant changes of players' positions as the team gain or lose possession of the ball. It is also called 'positionless soccer'. (Chyzowich 1978)

[11] West Germany won the World Cup in 1954 played in Switzerland. Ironically, they beat Hungary 4 - 2 in the final (Taylor and Jamrich, 1997).

[12] Sadly, for this study, Bill no longer has these letters in his possession.

[13] The term 'Busby Babes' is a popular reference to the pre-Munich Manchester United team, due to the fact they were so young.

[14] Wilf is referring here to the Association of Former Manchester United Players. The Association has regular events in order to raise funds for charity. The author is privileged to be a member.

[15] Wilf is referring here to youth tours in Switzerland, see Chapter Five.

**CHAPTER FIVE:
YOUTH CUP
COMPETITIONS**

This chapter will begin by tracing the history of youth football in England, and the origins of the Football Association Youth Cup competition. It will then go on to give a brief resume of the first five years of Manchester United's involvement in the FA Youth Cup (1953-57), a period germane to this study which is seeking to explain why Manchester United's youth policy during the fifties was so successful. The chapter will then examine and evaluate how the coaching and training methods which were discussed in the previous chapter were 'tested' in the realm of competition of this nature. The chapter will also seek to answer questions regarding the importance of youth tournaments in the developmental process of Manchester United's youth players during the period of this study. It will also explore the reason why they were so successful in winning the FA Youth Cup for the first five years of its existence (1953-57). The FA Youth Cup helped to broaden the players' experience by giving them the opportunity of playing against teams from different parts of the country rather than the local leagues they played in during their normal programme (see Chapter Three). The chapter will also attempt to answer the following questions: to what extent did the 'high profile' the Youth Cup brought (playing at Old Trafford for example) stimulate competition to get into the first team? In what ways did it prepare youth team players for first team football?

IN 1954 MANCHESTER UNITED were invited to play in an international youth tournament in Zurich, Switzerland. The chapter will examine the ways in which playing against foreign opposition in tournaments such as this assisted their football education: physically, technically, tactically, psychologically and socio-culturally. To what extent were trips abroad used by staff to instil club values and discipline? Themes which were discussed earlier.

During research, the author discovered an absence of documentary sources (other than statistical data) relating to the club's involvement in youth competition during the period of this study. I have relied heavily on the oral recollections of Terry Beckett and Wilf McGuinness whose testimony appears in previous chapters. Both Terry and Wilf's insights are invaluable, given the rarity of other sources to illuminate this aspect of Manchester United's history.

THE HISTORY OF YOUTH FOOTBALL

1926 saw the first efforts to bring youth football within the auspices of the Football Association. At that time the FA Council appointed a special committee to assess the prospect of assisting primary schools in developing football among schoolboys. The Committee also encouraged boys to join junior clubs until they were old enough to play with clubs at a more senior level. The Committee formulated rules for youth football and a special standing committee for junior football was appointed in July 1926. The following decade saw little progress and renewed efforts were made in the years 1936-39 following an FA survey. As a result of this, new leagues emerged nationally and there seemed to be a resolve to ensure that vital resources were put into youth football. It seemed that at last there was a realisation that if youngsters were looked after properly there would be a reservoir of promising players for both the amateur and professional game. Progress prior to the Second World War was steady and during the war youth football continued to flourish. In fact, in 1940 a national competition for youth teams was discussed. This resulted in an International Youth Tournament being organised in England under the jurisdiction of the Federation of Football Associations (FIFA), the game's governing body. Seven nations visited England for the Tournament which was held in London. The hosts won the inaugural tournament defeating Holland 3 - 2 in the final. This led to a programme of international youth tournaments as well as friendly matches which became quite extensive in scope.

Bobby Charlton, Duncan Edwards and Wilf McGuinness were all England Youth Internationals. The first national competition for youth players was launched in 1944 and became known as the FA County Youth Challenge Cup. As the title indicates, it was for representative teams of County Football Associations and only amateur players under the age of eighteen were eligible to play. This led to the inauguration of the FA Youth Challenge Cup Competition in 1952 which was to become such an important competition for Manchester United's youth policy in the fifties. (FABIAN AND GREEN 1960)

THE FA YOUTH CHALLENGE CUP COMPETITION, 1952-57

The introduction of the FA Youth Challenge Cup in 1952 was a further step towards bridging the gap between the school leaving age and senior football. Planning for the competition began at a meeting of the FA Council early in 1952 when Council member Joe Richards proposed a national competition for youth players between the age of fifteen and eighteen. The competition would be sponsored and controlled by the FA. Richards' proposal was accepted by the Council and a new FA standing committee was given full authority to proceed with the competition in season 1952-53. It was to be a knock-out competition for youth teams of football league clubs and other teams which were approved by the FA Council. Ninety-three clubs entered the competition in its inaugural season and they were grouped in geographical regions for convenience. Entrants included Manchester United, Wolverhampton Wanderers, West Bromwich Albion and Hereford Boys club. Manchester United proved invincible in the first five years of the competition. They demonstrated that they were able to maintain a consistently high level of play as the following statistics show:

MANCHESTER UNITED FA YOUTH CUP RECORD 1952-57	
GAMES PLAYED	46
GAMES WON	39
GAMES DRAWN	6
GAMES LOST	1
GOALS FOR	191
GOALS AGAINST	43
MOST CONSECUTIVE WINS	14

(Source: Cliff Butler MUFC)

Their first defeat did not come until 1957 when Southampton won 3 - 2 at Old Trafford in the second leg of the semi-final. However, they had won the first game at Southampton 5 - 2 to proceed to their fifth consecutive final. The first final was played at Old Trafford on 4th May 1953 against Wolves, United's great rivals in the recruitment of good youth players (see Chapter Two). The match was played on a home and away basis and watched by a crowd of 21,000. United won 7 - 1. The second game was played at Wolverhampton on 9th May and ended in a 2 - 2 draw, United winning the trophy by an aggregate score of 9 - 3. The Manchester United youth team included four players who were to die at Munich a mere five years later: Eddie Colman, Duncan Edwards, David Pegg and Billy Whelan.

One of our interviewees, Albert Scanlon, also played in the first final. He was to suffer horrific injuries in the Munich disaster which had an adverse affect on his career. The success of the inaugural season of the cup and the welcome it received from clubs, players and spectators surpassed even the wildest dreams of its founders. Many of the matches attracted crowds of up to 10,000 so it was also a financial success. Football supporters who were used to watching league and cup matches involving senior players were pleasantly surprised at the ability and skills of these young players.

The second year of the competition saw the entry of such teams as White Rose of York, Battle Athletic of Reading, Longfleet St Mary's of Dorset and North Dorset Youth. The final was a repeat of the previous year, the teams drew the first match 4 - 4 at Wolves, but Manchester United retained the cup by winning 1 - 0 at Old Trafford - David Pegg scoring from the penalty spot. The attendance for this match was an astonishing 28,000 which amply illustrates how the Youth Cup had captured the public's imagination. In subsequent years United defeated West Bromwich Albion, Chesterfield and West Ham United in the final. A glimpse at the match programme for the 1956 final against Chesterfield (first leg) on 30th April shows that the two teams each contained a player who would become a World Cup Winner for England in 1966 - Bobby Charlton for United, and Gordon Banks, Chesterfield's goalkeeper. Banks was to make a save from Pelé of Brazil in the 1970 World Cup which many still regard as the finest ever seen. The Youth Cup certainly proved to be a good breeding ground for outstanding players.

Following their third win in 1955 the FA presented United with an inscribed plaque to commemorate the achievement. The club thought the achievement merited a photograph of the plaque in a first team programme on 28th January 1956. The plaque was recently on display at the Manchester United Museum.

THE ROLE OF THE FA YOUTH CUP IN PLAYER DEVELOPMENT

AT MANCHESTER UNITED 1952-57

<small>EDDIE COLMAN ACCEPTS THE 1955 FA YOUTH CUP</small>

Having discussed Manchester United's unrivalled success in the early years of the FA Youth Cup, we are now concerned with the dynamics that lay behind that success. In other words to analyse how Matt Busby and Jimmy Murphy used the FA Youth Cup as a vital instrument in the development of young players at the club during the fifties. In order to do this the oral testimony of Terry Beckett and Wilf McGuinness is crucial. Both men played for the club in the Youth Cup during the period of this study. In fact, McGuinness played in three consecutive Youth Cup finals 1954-56. Chapter One showed that from the beginning of his managership of Manchester United, Busby concentrated on developing a coherent youth policy at the club. The winning of the FA Youth Cup was evidence that the youth policy was producing the calibre of player able to play for the first team. Eamon Dunphy makes the following comment in this regard:

"Winning the FA Youth Cup was an important target for Busby and Jimmy Murphy. Facing criticism from shareholding supporters at United's AGM, Busby had made large claims about the future, asserting that the club had £200,000 worth of youngsters in the reserve and youth teams. He hoped the FA Youth Cup would substantiate this claim"

As Dunphy (1991) says, success in the FA Youth Cup would go far in convincing everyone at the club that the future was assured given the quality of the young players the youth policy was producing. Furthermore, the club would save an enormous amount of money in transfer fees over the years. Terry Beckett made the following observation on the importance of the Youth Cup in relation to the development of young players at the club during the fifties.

"The way it worked out in those days was, so it seemed, if you had a successful youth side, especially at United, that quite a number of that youth side would come through to the first team. In my particular day for example there was Duncan Edwards who was already an international and a youth player which had never happened before.

"There was Bobby Charlton, who became a world class player, Wilf McGuinness who played regularly for the first team until his injury and quite a few others like Eddie Colman, and they all became successful first division players. So I think the youth side of it very important because the way it developed here at United. But of course it was a bit unique that they won it five times running, but quite a number of players come from the youth team into the first team. I think it was like a stepping stone. It was a very competitive competition but if you could win the Youth Cup you had, presumably, the best youth side in the country" INTERVIEW

Beckett cites the fact that Edwards, Charlton and McGuinness all graduated from the youth team to become regular first team players at Manchester United. All three became full internationals, and in the case of Edwards, he was so outstanding that he played for England whilst still a youth team player. Beckett clearly felt that success in the youth team was a vital 'stepping stone' to first team football. However it must be remembered that not all the players who played in United's successful Youth Cup winning teams made the grade - the failure rate even at United was extremely high.

Wilf McGuinness has said that the Youth Cup gave the young players a benchmark to aim for - it was important as a measure of standards. The players wanted to be the best and "winning the Youth Cup proved that they were in fact the best". To win the Youth Cup for five years in succession was a remarkable achievement. The magnitude of this accomplishment is demonstrated by the fact that no other club has come close to emulating the achievement nearly fifty years on. Terry Beckett offers an interesting appraisal of how this feat was achieved:

> *"Obviously it wasn't easy to win it that many times from the start of the competition. But the way I saw it at United, they attempted to sign as many schoolboy internationals as possible because somehow the side would consist of three or four local lads and the rest of them would be from other parts of England, but they'd have played for England Boys quite a number of them. They were the best players in the country in my opinion. When they got into the youth side, the various lads, they didn't want to move out of it because they want to go right through to the final. The year I arrived, I came and played in the third year of winning the competition[1955].*

ALL THOSE HOURS OF HARD-WORK PAID OFF FOR JOE, THE MASTER PROCURER OF TALENT, AS HE GETS HIS HANDS ON SOME OF THE TROPHIES HE PLAYED AN INSTRUMENTAL PART IN WINNING

SPOT THE DIFFERENCE:
THE THREE-YEAR ELIGIBILITY RULE MEANT THAT UNITED YOUTH'S TEAM HAD CONTINUITY - A CENTRAL FACTOR IN THE CLUB SETTING A RECORD OF FIVE CONSECUTIVE TRIUMPHS FROM THE START OF THE TOURNAMENT
PICTURED ARE TEAMS FROM 1954 (ABOVE), 1955 (OPPOSITE PAGE TOP) & 1957 (BELOW) - CAN YOU SPOT THE FAMILIAR FACES?

"It had been won the two years previous and a lot of the lads were schoolboy internationals, and you always had four, five or sometimes six who could play the following year at least. So you had a start on other teams and I think that's a big thing in the Youth Cup, I think it would be a big thing today. In other words if a lad came from England Boys at fifteen years of age he should be set off in the youth team so that he can play in that competition another two years which gives you a big advantage."

Beckett thought that the major reason for United's sustained success in the Youth Cup was the quality of the players that came to the club from schoolboy football. In other words, the scouting system under Joe Armstrong (see Chapter Two) was doing a fine job of bringing to the club some of the most promising schoolboy players in the country - many of them schoolboy internationals. Beckett also believed that the three-year eligibility rule was an important factor which helped to explain United's success. This meant that talented schoolboy players could play in the Youth Cup for three years. In this regard an article in a programme for a first team match on 22nd October 1955 is enlightening stating that:

"Once more the FA Youth Cup competition is upon us and the question arises 'can our boys do the near impossible by winning again the trophy they have held for the past three years?' Of last year's team no less than seven will be eligible to play again these being : Hawksworth, Queenan, Jones, McGuinness, Beckett, Charlton and Fidler. With English and Morgans (who played in several of the rounds) and recent schoolboy signings including three England Boys and several Manchester and Salford Boys being available, there is sure to be keen competition for places."

United during this period were also fortunate to have at their disposal the talent of Bobby Charlton and Duncan Edwards. This was a major reason they were able to dominate the Youth Cup for so many years. Edwards' talent was extraordinary, and with him in the team United were simply unbeatable. Great credit is due to Joe Armstrong for bringing such formidable talent to United at this time (see Chapter Two). It should also be remembered that the coaching and training the players were receiving on Tuesday and Thursday nights at the Cliff (see Chapter Four) would improve their skills and tactical knowledge thus making them even better players than they were at school.

Another factor was that the Youth Cup gave United's youth players the opportunity to play against players within their own age bracket which they did not do during their normal programme (see Chapter Three).

Wilf McGuinness firmly believed that winning the Youth Cup was evidence that United's youth policy was working at the time:

> *"Obviously Manchester United's youth policy was working because they played many teenagers in the first team in the fifties. If you look back on how many teenagers made their debuts for Manchester United - well a dozen, over a dozen, there were probably over twenty in the fifties."* INTERVIEW

Many of the players McGuinness mentions (himself included) would have graduated through the FA Youth Cup team.

We saw in Chapter Two that United had rivals in the sphere of youth development notably Wolverhampton Wanderers who United played in the first two Youth Cup finals. However, the evidence shows that United's policy was superior to any other in the country because they won the Youth Cup for five consecutive years and they got so many teenagers into the first team. In fact United's success in producing players for the first team via a youth policy in the fifties has only recently been emulated under Sir Alex Ferguson's management.

A HIGHER PROFILE

So how did the FA Youth Cup help to broaden the players' experience? A key part of the youth players' experience was the opportunity to play against teams from other parts of the country. It has been noted that United's junior players played all their football in local open age leagues. Yet to what extent did the "higher profile" Youth Cup stimulate competition to get into the team? Was it also a good preparation for the demands of first team football? According to Terry Beckett the experiences helped because,

> *"The semi-finals at Stamford Bridge against Chelsea [1955], final at West Brom [1955] - two-legged final - were played at these big grounds belonging to First*

Division sides. The odd games against teams like Barnsley, they put up a tremendous fight against us... but I think it stands you in good stead playing on First Division grounds. For instance there were between 15 and 20,000 watching us at Stamford Bridge...

"When I walked out on to the pitch before a big crowd I kind of thrived on it, I loved it. I think it was a big thing because they got a good judgement of you playing against other First Division sides. The youth competition itself was a great idea because you got the best in England at under eighteen and therefore you knew you were playing against the best in England at that age, and if you won the competition you could take it that you were the best. And I think we were because we won it so many times... I think it stood us in really good stead, yes, that's my opinion. Cause once you got into the youth team you were then expecting you'd be playing in the 'A' team and then you'd be expecting a place in the reserves if you were doing well in the youth side and so on." INTERVIEW

Beckett emphasises the fact that playing on first division grounds in front of big crowds created the kind of 'big match' atmosphere that could not be considered during their normal programme. It also placed different demands on the players psychologically. The intensity of the competition helped the coaching staff to assess the extent of the players' ability to cope with the demands of playing at a higher level. Passing this test was an indication that a player was genuine first team material. The FA Youth Cup was a simulation of a first team game in a very real way according to Bobby Charlton, who made the following statement about what playing in the Youth Cup meant to the players:

"We won the Youth Cup every year I played - the first five years of its existence it was won by Manchester United. But the Youth team, as Jimmy Murphy used to say, was the cream of Manchester United. This was the most important thing. Forget about the first team and the FA Cup and all that - this is the most important thing. And I can remember I wouldn't go to bed the night before a youth match because I'd been brainwashed, indoctrinated into thinking that this was the most important match that you ever played in your whole life." VIDEO *Official History of Manchester United* (1998)

Charlton's comment gives an indication of just how important the club considered the Youth Cup to be - a microcosm of a first team game. A regular place in the youth team placed a player quite high on the ladder towards reserve and ultimately first team football. Thus for Busby and Murphy it was an important aspect of a player's development. Wilf McGuinness said the following with regard to the juxtaposition of Youth Cup and first team football:

"The crowds that we got on a normal game were nothing in comparison, but by the time we were still youth team players a lot of us had played in the first team in front of forty and fifty thousand. I played as a 17-year-old in Manchester United's first team, Bobby as an 18-year-old, Duncan as a 16-year-old, David Pegg, Albert Scanlon had both played as 17-year-olds in Manchester United's first team as well as Bill Whelan. These players had all experienced big crowds and experienced playing with current internationals.

"But we also experienced playing on bad pitches in local leagues. We did win some of those eight and nine nil. The tougher ones like the Wythenshawe teams who had tough lads in, we'd win 3 - 1 and 2 - 1. But mainly it was playing against weaker opposition that helped us. We were good players to start with I must tell you. Obviously they didn't sign many bad players United - but what I'm trying to get over is we developed the confidence and the team spirit by winning - winning things - not by losing things by winning that's how we got the bonding.

"But it wasn't like a first team game - first team football is first team football it's not like the reserves... There's nothing like playing in the first team, but like I've mentioned what it did do, it got us the team spirit and it got us Manchester United minded... because of winning, the club winning, the team winning. It's not only 'you're my pal - we're all under one umbrella which is Manchester United'. But it got us, most of us anyway, so that we would want to give everything not only to the team but to the name of Manchester United because Jimmy Murphy, if we did something

wrong he'd say, 'you're going against Manchester United' like you were going against each other. 'You're going against Manchester United' or if you're doing well, 'you're doing it for Manchester United'.

"So Jimmy would remind us, 'You're representing Manchester United...you're not representing Bobby Charlton, Wilf McGuinness, Duncan Edwards, Eddie Colman... you're representing Manchester United. You're not representing me you know' - that was how he put it over. That came through above everything in my opinion, that we were representing Manchester United, I felt like that anyway - I was doing it for Manchester United.

"It was the experience you gained by playing before big crowds, representing the club with people watching and proving to everybody that you wanted to be a player yourself. But the difference I found with youth football - and I was top notch in a way - I'd captained England Youth and I was on my way up and everything. But playing in the first team at Manchester United was a lot more difficult. Not difficult because we had good players to play with, that was the important thing. But I wasn't in the game as much, I still had a lot to learn at that level. Other players were in the game far more because they were more experienced - you can't beat experience. Until I got that experience, it did come, I found I wasn't doing as much in a first team game as I was in a youth team game." INTERVIEW

Again McGuinness mentions the grounds and the size of the crowds they played in front of, this gave the Youth Cup games a much higher profile. However, when comparing games in the youth team with first team football, he does place things in perspective. He states that players who had played in the first team (including himself) at a young age did not find the big grounds and crowds as daunting as it may have been for some of the opposing players. This would obviously give Manchester United a big advantage when they played against teams whose players did not have this experience. This is probably another reason why they won the Youth Cup so consistently.

Playing on park pitches also helped to refine technique, and playing against weaker opponents helped the players to build confidence by winning games. Thus these junior games could be seen as preparation for the more challenging competition the Youth Cup provided. However, McGuinness makes the important point that no matter how good the Youth Cup was in terms of preparing players for first team football, it was not a substitute for 'the real thing'. He admits he had much to learn at that level, and in fact could not get into the game enough. First team football had its own demands - demands that eclipsed the competition the Youth Cup provided.

It is interesting that McGuinness makes reference to the fact that winning matches was extremely important even at youth level because it helped to build confidence as well as team spirit. The players were not simply playing for themselves, but rather they were playing for each other as well as the good name of Manchester United. Having pride in the club was an important value which was instilled in the players, as noted earlier.

THE F.C. BLUE
STARS YOUTH
TOURNAMENT

On 26th May 1954 Manchester United's youth team travelled to Zurich, Switzerland, to compete in an international youth tournament. This was the first time an English club had competed in a competition of this nature. The author has been privileged to handle Wilf McGuinness's itinerary for the tour (right), one of only a handful still in existence. It is a remarkable document and its production is evidence of how important the trip was considered to be. The tour party consisted of the following staff:

J.A. Gibson (Director)

M. Busby (Manager)

J. Murphy (Coach)

B. Whalley (Coach)

PLAYERS

I. Beswick	E. Lewis
R. Charlton	T. Littler
G. Clayton	W. McGuinness
E. Colman	P. Pearce
D. Edwards	D. Pegg
B. Fulton	A. Rhodes
T. Hawksworth	A. Scanlon
R. Harrop	W. Whelan

TRAINER

A. Powell

The competition was completed in a single day (Thursday 27th May) and Manchester United's youth team won. Following the Tournament, the team played a series of 'friendly matches' against Swiss youth teams, one of which was played before an international match between Switzerland and the Netherlands. The total length of the trip was seven days (26th May - 1st June 1954). It proved to be a wonderful educational experience for the young players both on and off the field.

The importance of the tournament for Busby is demonstrated by the presence of the club's senior coaching staff on the trip: Busby, Murphy and Whalley. James Gibson, a director, was also in attendance. It is clear from this that Busby and Murphy saw the visit to Zurich as an important step in the players' development. Given the absence of formal records of the trips to Switzerland during the period of this study, oral testimony is extremely important in order to find out, from the players who were there, how the trips to Europe assisted the players' education: technically, tactically, physically and socially. To what extent were they used to instill club values and discipline? Bobby Charlton had said the following about the value of playing in Europe as a youth player:

> "The Tournament was a vital part of our education. We played against Italians, Germans and Yugoslavs and learned about their different ways of playing. We went three years on the trot and won the first two tournaments. Then we lost 1 - 0 to Genoa in the final. They never came out of their own half once, and we thought 'there's something not right here'. We'd never encountered anything like this at home. But they knew what they were doing, defending in typical Italian style. They wouldn't let you past, it was frustrating but an amazing education." (DUNPHY 1991)

Wilf McGuinness, who also went on the first trip, testifies to the value of the experience and during interview he had the following to say:

> "Psychologically we knew we were playing in a different country, different styles, different players. We had players playing from Italy, you know, against us. Italian teams, German teams, Swiss teams, French all this came into it. And we found it didn't bother us that much even though most teams had a sweeper who played very deep in those days, you know, which we never had in England. But we had quality players like Bobby Charlton in the team and before that of course the great Duncan and players like

that. So we played to our qualities. But we found, even then, they had a lot of skilled players. I mean we played against the Italians - Genoa who had wonderful players. We played against Augsburg and they had Haller who turned out to be a star player for Germany. I marked him and I can always remember him picking up the ball in, I think it was the final. We played on the good pitch - you know the very good pitch at Zurich instead of the junior pitches we played some of the Tournament games on. And the crowd had seen him previously, and there was a big 'Oh!' as he picked up the ball. Then he dropped his shoulder - sold me a brilliant dummy and I went the wrong way, and I thought 'Oh! that's why!' But he only did it once! But playing against those sort of players, it gave you the experience as well. There we were playing against their best youth team players and it was tremendous...

"Some of the things that stuck in my mind about the Blue Stars Tournament was it wasn't unusual to play several games in a day you know - twenty minutes each way or whatever the system was - and then the final. But it was going together as friends and going around cities, and having new experiences - like they had the trams in Zurich where we didn't have trams here in those days. They were on the right-hand side of the road. These were things that stuck in our minds and experiences. Seeing various things and trying to explain to people where we wanted to go in a foreign language...

"I always tell that story in the hotel that they put lettuce on a side plate and I didn't know if you should eat it before the meal, during or after you know and things like that. And our first 'creme caramel' - what is this like? These kinds of cultural experiences bring out the confidence in you when you handle the situation. Like what certain things mean in different languages, or the way to behave abroad. And the duvets, we didn't have duvets. I always remember - what's this on the bed? Where's the blankets? They grew up differently in certain things they did and we had to learn how to adapt: when in Rome do what the Romans do. So these were all learning processes which stuck in my mind...

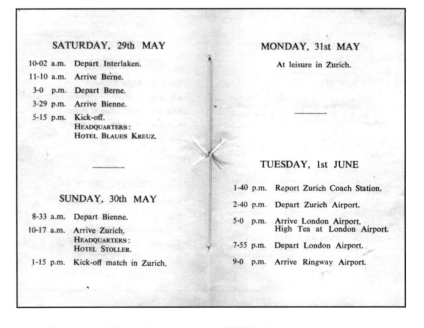

PAGES FROM UNITED'S TOUR ITINERARY 1954. AS THE PRODUCTION OF THIS BOOK SUGGESTS, THE CLUB TOOK THE TOURNAMENT VERY SERIOUSLY

"When I was England schoolboy captain, we stayed in a couple of hotels but it was easier in English hotels than in foreign hotels. It was a big experience, having shutters on your windows – it was all part of growing up." INTERVIEW

McGuinness comments that in Europe the players had to adjust to different styles of play so they had to be strong mentally. However, he considered that they had good enough players to cope with the demands the tournament placed on them. Charlton and Edwards were quality players even at this stage of their development.

The one tactical innovation that was different was the Continentals' use of the 'sweeper system' which involved one of the team's defenders playing 'deeper' behind the other defenders in order to 'sweep-up' any dangerous balls that got past them. Bobby Charlton also noted the Continentals' ultra-defensive style. McGuinness describes many of the foreign players as 'wonderful' so they were obviously very accomplished players - making United's achievement of winning the tournament two years in succession a considerable feat. McGuinness makes specific reference to the German player Haller who made a big impression on him. He was an exciting player as well as being a crowd pleaser. He had the aesthetic qualities so admired by Busby. It is interesting to note that Haller was to play in the 1966 World Cup Final for West Germany against England at Wembley, scoring a goal in his country's 4 - 2 defeat. Appearing for England was, of course, Bobby Charlton whom he had played against in the Blue Stars Tournament twelve years before.

Playing against players of Haller's ilk gave the young United players tremendous experience - the Blue Stars Tournament was clearly a superb breeding ground for players as the above example shows. Playing against the best players in Europe and beating them was an enormous confidence booster for the players. McGuinness describes the unusual nature of the Blue Stars Tournament in which the players had to play several games in a single day - including the final. This meant that the players had to be physically and mentally strong in order to meet all the demands of the day.

McGuinness also stresses the importance of the trips to Europe in cementing friendships between the players as well as providing a cultural education. The ability to adapt to different languages and cultures could only help the players to develop self-confidence which in turn assisted their development as aspiring footballers. So to what extent did Wilf think the trips to Europe were used to instil club values and discipline?

We had a curfew. I was captain one time and I always remember being a little bit late, breaking it, and Arthur Powell on the stairs and giving us 'hey what's going on?' And you know, all right come on we've overstepped the mark here. These things they'd happen occasionally but nothing too severe obviously. But it was part of the growing-up process and the team spirit and the bonding." INTERVIEW

It was noted in Chapter Three that standards of discipline were not overly strict and in general the players were expected to behave responsibly and use their common sense. It would seem that when on tour a similar attitude to discipline prevailed. McGuinness felt that the occasional misdemeanour and the resultant pulling into line 'hey what's going on' was a means of generating team spirit and helped to bond the players tightly together. A bit of mischief was an integral part of the growing-up process as players.

It is clear from all this that the experience of playing in Europe was a tremendous benefit to the young players at Manchester United in the fifties. It is intriguing to contemplate the extent to which the experiences of the youth team in Switzerland influenced Busby's decision to enter the European Cup in 1956. On this point McGuinness has the following to say:

"Well, with Matt Busby going and watching, we went in 1954, and there was one game we played before the Dutch team played against the Swiss team. I'm sure with Matt Busby watching it and thinking, 'well this is where we've got to be'. I'm sure that was in his mind - this is where Manchester United have got to be. The crowd, the experience and the success we were having I'm sure he felt this was the way forward for the club. And it was possibly watching Manchester United perform against these clubs abroad that pushed him into later decisions."

The author is convinced that Busby's presence in Zurich in 1954 for the youth tour was an affirmation that he believed that the future of English football lay in embracing what European football had to offer. The Blue Stars Youth Tournament was a golden opportunity to 'test the waters' and he wanted to be there to witness it personally. The 1954 visit to Switzerland by the youth team established a club tradition of going to the Blue Stars Tournament which persists today. Indeed the youth team celebrated the 50th anniversary of the club attending the tournament with a victory in 2004. On a personal

THE WINNING TEAM:
UNITED PROVED THE HEALTH OF THEIR YOUTH POLICY BY WINNING THE BLUE STARS TOURNAMENT IN 1954. THE FOLLOWING YEAR THEY LOST 0-1 TO GENOA. HOWEVER, THE EXPLOITS OF THE YOUTH TEAM CLEARLY GAVE BUSBY FOOD FOR THOUGHT AND WHEN UNITED WERE INVITED INTO THE EUROPEAN CUP HE HAD LITTLE HESITATION IN ACCEPTING.

note, I was privileged to go on three such trips (1969, 1971 and 1972) when I was a youth player at the club. Thus I have personal experience of just how valuable such trips were for a player's development.

In 1955 the European Cup was inaugurated. As is widely known, Chelsea, the English Champions, did not enter on the advice of the Football League who felt that this new venture was unimportant and they should concentrate on the domestic programme in England. In 1956, against the protestations of the Football League, Manchester United entered the European Cup. With an extremely young and exciting team, dubbed 'the Busby Babes' by an adoring public, they reached the semi-finals for two years in succession. This was a remarkable achievement for such a young side. Sadly, however,

the tragedy of the Munich disaster in February 1958 left the enormous potential of those wonderful players unfulfilled.

It was Busby's vision in taking the youth side to Europe in 1954 that paved the way to the success of the pre-Munich team and ultimately to the club's success in winning the trophy in 1968 - the pinnacle of Busby's magnificent managerial achievements. It must not be forgotten that for many of the pre-Munich team: Charlton, Colman, Edwards, Scanlon, going into Europe was not a new phenomenon, they had been there before, competing against the best teams in Europe in the Blue Stars Tournament in Zurich. The experience was to stand them in good stead for the challenges of playing in Europe at senior level.

To summarise, then, the FA Youth Cup was seen by Matt Busby and Jimmy Murphy as a means of developing the youth policy at Manchester United in the fifties. It broadened the players' experience by giving them the opportunity of testing themselves against teams from other parts of the country in large stadiums in front of big crowds. It also served as a means of sharpening the players' competitive edge as well as inculcating a large degree of team spirit, discipline and pride in the football club. The ventures to Europe exposed them to different styles of play as well as being a sound cultural education.

Youth Cup competitions in England and Europe contributed to Busby and Murphy's desire to expose the youth players at Manchester United to the intense competition that would help prepare them for their first team football. It would also give them the opportunity to express themselves creatively and aesthetically in accord with Busby's philosophy of football which were discussed in Chapters One, Three and Four of this study. Furthermore, the competition for places in the youth team raises issues with regard to conflict and conflict resolution which were set forth by Elias and Dunning (1971).

CONCLUSION

The principle aim of this study was to analyse the reasons why Manchester United's youth policy during the fifties was so successful. During this period United won the FA Youth Cup for five consecutive years (1953-1957) and produced some outstanding players such as Duncan Edwards and Bobby Charlton. Edwards' career was tragically cut short by the Munich disaster, but Charlton became a player of great distinction. The introduction explains why the author chose to use oral history and interview techniques as opposed to other research methods such as questionnaires.

The literature review in Chapter One included an analysis of what has been written about the social history of football in general and Manchester United in particular by historians of football: Young (1960), Walvin (1975 and Mason (1980) placing the research within a sound historical framework. It also showed that sociologists and educationalists have developed theories about sport (including football) and these were examined to show which of them had particular relevance to the study. Three theories were considered to be important: the configurational sociology of Dunning (1971); Huizinga's (1970) theories of play and Keller's (Whitings and Masterson 1974) aesthetic concepts in relation to football.

It goes on to explain that when Matt Busby arrived as manager of the Club in 1945 a youth policy had already been established for many years. However, through his energy and vision he transformed the youth policy into a vibrant, cohesive, dynamic and systematic programme which epitomised his own philosophy of football. In other words he created a culture at the football club which elevated the importance of youth to a level that had never been seen before at a football club in England. It is true that other clubs had developed youth policies during this time, notably Wolverhampton Wanderers under the managership of Stan Cullis - but other clubs did not produce the quality of players through their youth policy that Busby did at Manchester United.

Chapter Two showed that from the beginning of his management Busby placed great emphasis on having a quality scouting system in order to recruit the finest young schoolboy footballers for Manchester United. He did not employ many scouts around the country, but those he did were excellent judges of talent. The scouting network was led by Joe Armstrong, the Chief Scout, who was responsible for signing many of the most promising schooboy players in the country. Armstrong had a magnetic personality and the ability to convince players and their parents that Manchester United would give them an opportunity to play in the first team. The Club would also take an active interest in the general welfare of their sons because they were a 'family club'. Armstrong was also extremely astute at forging good relations with the Schools Football Associations who controlled schoolboy football as well as access to players.

In Chapter Three we saw that after joining the Club as amateurs, the youth players trained on two nights a week: Tuesday and Thursday. They could not sign professional forms for the Club until they were seventeen so until then they had to get jobs with local firms or join the Club's groundstaff. Those who wished to go to college fulltime to study for academic or vocational qualifications. On Saturday they played for one of the junior teams hoping to progress ultimately to the first team. The programme was demanding, and even if they signed professional forms the pay was not especially good. The attraction of professional football was the opportunity to eventually play in front of huge crowds and be hero-worshipped by devoted supporters. Money was a secondary consideration.

The chapter also showed that Busby took a great interest in the young players at Manchester United. He knew that many of them had left their families to come to Manchester to ply their trade in football and he felt a profound responsibility for their welfare. He himself had left home at an early age and had felt the loneliness of being away from hearth and home. He was thus extremely sensitive to their needs. Busby tried to make Manchester United a second family to them instilling in them a sense of belonging, loyalty, decency and respect for one another. This 'bonding' process was the only way he could produce the kind of player he wanted at Manchester United. Busby's attempt to create a 'family club' at Manchester United sprang also from his own upbringing in a mining village in Scotland where a spirit of family and community was important, given the harsh demands of working life. Losing his father in the first world war made him the family 'breadwinner' at an early age engendering in him a sense of paternalism, a desire to properly 'look after' the young boys in his charge.

Professional football was a demanding business with competition for places on the team creating its own tensions. It was argued that because relationships between the young players was good this helped to alleviate such tensions so that the working relationships between the players produced harmony rather than conflict (Dunning 1971). We saw in Chapter Four that the coaching and training at the Club concentrated on teaching the young players Busby's philosophy of football. That is, his belief that football should be played in a creative, instinctive way. Playing for the team was vital, but just as important was individual expression, invention and flair. In short, Busby was seeking to produce players who possessed aesthetic qualities. In order to do this the players were not over-coached - they were not restricted by tactical regimentation. In that sense Busby was applying, however unwittingly, Huizinga's (1970) theory of play which stressed the importance of free expression in the development of sport and culture.

The chapter demonstrated that the coaching of youth at Manchester United was the responsibility of Jimmy Murphy, Busby's assistant. Murphy was an outstanding coach and motivator of young players and was a major reason why the Club's youth policy in the fifties was so successful. Busby was not afraid to look abroad for new ideas and he greatly admired the aesthetic style of play the Hungarian team displayed when beating England at Wembley in 1953.

Finally, in Chapter Five we looked at the FA Youth Cup which was inaugurated in 1952. It was an important means for Busby to test the development of the players in a high profile youth tournament. Winning the competition for five years in succession was proof that Manchester United's youth policy during the fifties was pre-eminent. Many of the players who featured in the FA Youth Cup winning teams went on to have distinguished careers at the Club.

The youth team also played in the FC Blue Stars Tournament in Zurich, Switzerland which was another important aspect of their development. The experience of playing in tournaments like this exposed them to different styles of play as well as providing valuable cultural education. This helped the players to mature more quickly which in turn assisted their development as footballers. In the long term it proved to be a wonderful preparation for the time when the Club entered the European Cup in 1956 and as we know they eventually went on to win this trophy twice in 1968 and 1999.

STATISTICS – MANCHESTER UNITED IN THE FA YOUTH CUP 1952-57

FA YOUTH CUP 1952-53

Round	Opposition	Venue		Result
1st round	Leeds United	Home		4-0
2nd round	Nantwich Town	Home		23-0
3rd round	Bury	Home		2-0
4th round	Everton	Home		1-0
5th round	Barnsley	Home		3-1
Semi-Final	Brentford	(1st Leg) Away		2-1
		(2nd Leg) Home		6-0

All statistics courtesy of
Cliff Butler, Statistician,
Manchester United FC

FINAL : 1st leg - Wolves (H) Won : 7-1

United: Clayton, Fulton, Kennedy, Colman, Cope, Edwards, McFarlane, Whelan, Lewis. Pegg, Scanlon.

Scorers: McFarlane (2), Lewis (2), Pegg, Scanlon, Whelan.

FINAL : 2nd leg - Wolves (A) Drawn 2-2

United: As 1st leg

Scorers: Lewis, Whelan

FA YOUTH CUP 1953-54

Round	Opposition	Venue		Result
1st round	Everton	Away		1-0
2nd round	Wrexham	Home		5-0
3rd round	Bradford PA	Home		6-0
4th round	Rotherham Utd	Away		0-0
	replay	Home		3-1
5th round	Bexley Heath	Home		2-1
Semi-Final	West Bromwich	(1st Leg)	Away	3-1
	Albion	(2nd Leg)	Home	4-0

FINAL: 1st leg - Wolves (H) Drew 4-4

United: Hawksworth, Beswick, Rhodes, Colman, Harrop, McGuinness, Littler, Edwards, Charlton, Pegg, Scanlon.

Scorers: Edwards (2), Pegg (2)

FINAL: 2nd leg - Wolves (A) Won 1-0

United: As 1st leg

Scorer: Pegg (pen)

FA YOUTH CUP 1954-55

Round	Opposition	Venue		Result
1st round	Liverpool	Away		4-1
2nd round	Manchester City	Away		2-1
3rd round	Barnsley	Away		4-2
4th round	Sheffield Wed	Home		7-0
5th round	Plymouth Argyle	Home		2-1
Semi-Final	Chelsea	(1st Leg) Away		2-1
		(2nd Leg) Home		2-1

FINAL: 1st leg - West Bromwich Albion (H) won 4-1

United: Hawksworth, Queenan, Rhodes, Colman, Jones, McGuinness, Beckett, Brennan, Edwards, Charlton, Fidler.

Scorers: Colman 2, Charlton, Beckett

2ND leg - West Bromwich Albion (A) won 3-0

United: As 1st leg

Scorer: Charlton, Edwards, own goal

FA YOUTH CUP 1955-56

Round	Opposition	Venue		Result
1st round		Bye		
2nd round	Preston North End	Away		5-2
3rd round	Sunderland	Home		4-0
4th round	Newcastle United	Home		7-1
5th round	Bexley Heath	Home		11-1
Semi-Final	Bolton Wanderers	(1st Leg)	Away	1-1
		(2nd Leg)	Home	3-0

FINAL: 1ST LEG - CHESTERFIELD (H) WON 3-2

United: Hawksworth, Queenan, Jones, Carolan, Holland, McGuinness, Morgans, Pearson, Dawson, Charlton, Fidler.

Scorers: Pearson, Charlton, Carolan.

2ND LEG - CHESTERFIELD (A) 1-1

United: As 1st leg

Scorer: Fidler

FA YOUTH CUP 1956-57

Round	Opposition	Venue		Result
1st round	Burnley	Home		5-2
2nd round	Huddersfield Town	Away		4-2
3rd round	Sunderland	Home		3-1
4th round	Everton	Away		2-2
Replay		Home		5-2
5th round	Blackburn Rovers	Home		6-0
Semi-Final	Southampton	(1st Leg)	Away	5-2
		(2nd Leg)	Home	2-3

FINAL: 1ST LEG - WEST HAM UNITED (A) WON 3-2

United: Gaskell, Smith, Maddison, English, Holland, Bratt, Morgans, Lawton, Dawson, Pearson, Hunter.

Scorers: Dawson, Pearson, Hunter

2ND LEG - WEST HAM UNITED (H) WON 5-0

United: As 1st leg

Scorers: Pearson 2, Dawson 2, Hunter

MANCHESTER UNITED'S OVERALL RECORD IN YOUTH TOURNAMENTS

FA YOUTH CUP

WINNERS (9): 1953, 1954, 1955, 1956, 1957, 1964, 1992, 1995, 2003
RUNNERS-UP (3): 1982, 1986, 1993
SEMI-FINALISTS (9): 1958, 1959, 1960, 1970, 1980, 1981, 1990, 1991.

BLUE STARS TOURNAMENT

WINNERS (17): 1954, 1957, 1959, 1960, 1961, 1962, 1965, 1966, 1968, 1975, 1976, 1978, 1979, 1981, 1982, 2004
RUNNERS-UP (8): 1955, 1964, 1971, 1973, 1974, 1991, 1992, 1994
THIRD PLACE (4): 1970, 1988, 1993, 1995.

BIBLIOGRAPHY

Busby, Matt and Jack, David (1957) My Story, London: Souvenir Press.

Busby, Matt and Fryer, Bill (1973), Soccer at the Top, London: Weidenfield and Nicholson.

Butler, Cliff and Ponting Ivan (1999), Manchester United Official Yearbook 1999, London: Manchester United Books.

Cashmore, Ellis (1990), Making Sense of Sport, London: Routledge.

Caunce, Stephen (1994), Oral History and the Local Historian, London: Longman.

Charlton, Bobby (1967), Forward for England, London: The Sportsman's Book Club.

Chzowych, Walter (1978), The Official Soccer Book of the United States Soccer Federation, New York: Rand McNally and company.

Clarke, Alf (1951), Manchester United, London: Convoy.

Coakley, Jay (1994), Sport in Society: Issues and Controversies, St Louis: Mosby.

Csandi, Arpad (1963), Soccer, Budapest: Corvino Press.

Dunning, Eric (Ed.) (1971), The Sociology of Sport: A Selection of Readings, London: Frank Cass.

Dunning, Eric, Murphy, Patrick and Williams, John (1988), The Roots of Football Hooliganism, London: Routledge and Keegan Paul.

Dunphy, Eamon and Ball, Peter (1986) Only a Game: The Diary of a Professional Footballer Harmondsworth: Viking.

Dunphy, Eamon (1991), Sir Matt Busby and Manchester United: A Strange Kind of Glory, London: Heinemann.

Dykes, Garth (1994), The United Alphabet, Leicester: A.C.L. Colour Print and Solar Publishing.

Edwards, Duncan (1958), Tackle Soccer this Way, London: Stanley Paul.

Elias, Norbert and Dunning, Eric, (1986), Quest for Excitement, Sport and Leisure in the Civilising Process, Oxford: Basil Blackwell.

Elias, Norbert (1994), The Civilising Process, Oxford: Basil Blackwell.

Fabian, A.H. and Green, Geoffrey (Eds.) (1960), Association Football, 4 Vols, London: Caxton Publishing Company.

Ferguson, Alex and McIlvanney, Hugh (1999) Managing My Life: My Autobiography, London: Hodder and Stoughton.

Fishwick, Nicholas (1989) English Football and Society 1910-1950, Manchester: Manchester University Press.

Glanville, Rick, (1994), Sir Matt Busby: A Tribute, London: Virgin Publishing.

Green, Geoffrey (1974), Soccer in the Fifties, London: Ian Allen.

Green, Geoffrey (1978), There's only One United : The Official History of Manchester United, London: Hodder and Stoughton.

Gutmann, Allen (1986), Sports Spectators, New York: Columbia University Press.

Hopcraft, Arthur (1968), The Football Man: People and Passions in Soccer, London: Collins.

HUGHES, CHARLES (1973), SOCCER TACTICS AND TEAMWORK, WAKEFIELD: E.P. PUBLISHINNG.

HUGHES, CHARLES (1980), THE FOOTBALL ASSOCIATION COACHING BOOK OF SOCCER TACTICS AND SKILLS, HARPENDEN, HERTS: QUEENE ANNE PRESS.

HUGHES, CHARLES (1990), THE WINNING FORMULA : SOCCER SKILLS AND TACTICS, LONDON: COLLINS.

HUIZINGA, JOHAN (1970) HOMO LUDENS: A STUDY OF THE PLAY ELEMENT IN CULTURE, LONDON: TEMPLE SMITH.

KENNEDY, MICHAEL (1980), THE CONCISE OXFORD DICTIONARY OF MUSIC, OXFORD : OXFORD UNIVERSITY PRESS.

LOVEJOY, JOE (1998), BESTIE: PORTRAIT OF A LEGEND, LONDON: SIDGEWICK AND JACKSON.

MARSHALL, GORDON (ED.) (1994), THE CONCISE OXFORD DICTIONARY OF SOCIOLOGY, OXFORD: OXFORD UNIVERSITY PRESS.

MARWICK, ARTHUR (1970), THE NATURE OF HISTORY, LONDON: MACMILLAN PRESS.

MARWICK, ARTHUR (1982), BRITISH SOCIETY SINCE 1945, LONDON: PENGUIN.

MASON, TONY (1980), ASSOCIATION FOOTBALL AND ENGLISH SOCIETY 1863 - 1915, SUSSEX: HARVESTER PRESS.

MEEK, DAVID AND TYRRELL, TOM (1997), THE HAMLYN ILLUSTRATED HISTORY OF MANCHESTER UNITED 1878 - 1979 LONDON: REED INTERNATIONAL BOOKS.

MEISL, WILLY (1955), SOCCER REVOLUTION LONDON: PHOENIX SPORTS BOOKS.

MILES, BARRY (1997), PAUL MCCARTNEY: MANY YEARS FROM NOW, LONDON: KECKER AND WARBURG.

MILLER, DAVID (1994), FATHER OF FOOTBALL: THE STORY OF SIR MATT BUBSY, LONDON: PAVILION BOOKS.

MORRIS, DESMOND (1981), THE SOCCER TRIBE, LONDON: JONATHAN CAPE.

MURPHY, JIMMY AND TAYLOR, FRANK (1968), MATT...UNITED... AND ME, LONDON: SOUVENIR PRESS.

MCINTOSH, PETER (1963), SPORT IN SOCIETY, LONDON: C.A. WATTS AND COMPANY.

ROBERTS (1975), THE TEAM THAT WOULDN'T DIE: THE STORY OF THE BUSBY BABES, LONDON: ARTHUR BAKER.

SEDDON, PETER (1995), A FOOTBALL COMPENDIUM: A COMPLETE GUIDE TO THE LITERATURE IN FOOTBALL, THE BRITISH LIBRARY: WETHERBY, W YORKS.

TAYLOR, ROGAN AND WARD, ANDREW (1995), KICKING AND SCREAMING : AN ORAL HISTORY OF FOOTBALL IN ENGLAND, LONDON: ROBSON BOOKS.

TAYLOR, ROGAN AND JAMRICH, KLARA (EDS.) (1997), PUSKAS ON PUSKAS: THE LIFE AND TIMES OF A FOOTBALL LEGEND, LONDON: ROBSON BOOKS.

THOMPSON, PAUL (1978), THE VOICE OF THE PAST: ORAL HISTORY, OXFORD: OXFORD UNIVERSITY PRESS.

WADE, ALLEN (1967), THE FOOTBALL ASSOCIATION GUIDE TO TRAINING AND COACHING, LONDON: HEINEMANN.

WALVIN, JAMES (1975), THE PEOPLE'S GAME: A SOCIAL HISTORY OF BRITISH FOOTBALL, LONDON: ALLEN LANE.

WHITING H.T.A. AND MASTERSON D.W. (EDS.) (1974), READINGS IN THE AESTHETICS OF SPORT, LONDON: LEPUS BOOKS.

WINTERBOTTOM, WALTER (1952), SOCCER COACHING, KINGSWOOD, SURREY: NALDRETT PRESS.

YOUNG, PERCY (1960), MANCHESTER UNITED, LONDON: HEINEMANN.

Young, Percy (1968), *A History of British Football*, London: Stanley Paul.

Young, Percy (1976), *Centenary Wolves*, Wolverhampton: Wolverhampton Wanderers F.C.

Journal Articles

Kerrigan, Colm, "London Schoolboys and Professional Football, 1899-1915," *International Journal of the History of Sport*, 11,2 (August 1994).

Taylor, Rogan and Ward, Andrew, "Kicking and Screaming: Broadcasting Football Oral Histories", *Oral History*, 25, 1 (Spring, 1997).

Magazines, Brochures And Handbooks

The Charlton Boys : Bobby and Jack (1968), B.P.C. Publishing, London.

English Schools Football Association Handbook 1957-58 Joseph Wones, West Bromwich, Staffs.

Football Association Coaching Licence E.U.F.A. "A" Coaching Award, Study Pack 5 (The Football Association, 1996).

The Football Association Premier League Rules, Section M, Youth Development (1998).

Manchester Schools Football Association Bulletin, 1950.

Manchester Schools Football Association Handbooks 1946-1958, Stronach and Company, Eccles, Manchester.

Wilf McGuinness Testimonial Souvenir Brochure, Caldwells, Manchester.

Newspapers

Dublin Evening Herald (10.1.70), Guardian (27.4.99), Sunday Telegraph (4.2.73), Sunday Times (18.4.99)

Manchester United Museum And Archives Sources

Match Programmes: 1950 - 1957.

Player Contracts.

Player. Training Rules and Instruction Booklets, 1950-56.

Video: the Official History of Manchester United: 120 Years of Passion, Video Collection International, 1998.
Youth Team Memorabilia 1950-1957.

PRIVATE COLLECTIONS

Armstrong papers, Becket papers., Cassidy papers, McGuinness papers, Whelan papers.

LIST OF ILLUSTRATIONS AND PHOTOGRAPHS

Photographs courtesy of Wilf McGuinness, Joe Armstrong junior and the author.
Every effort has been made to trace copyright holders and we apologise in advance for any unintentional omission. We would be pleased to insert the appropriate acknowledgement in any subsequent edition.

INDEX

PLAYERS, MANAGERS etc.

McCloy, Phil, 55
McDougall, Jimmy, 56
McGuinness, Wilf, 4, 5, 7, 8, 33, 34, 35, 45, 46, 50, 58, 62, 69, 70, 71, 72, 73, 78, 79, 80, 81, 82, 83, 84, 88, 89, 92, 93, 94, 95, 97, 98, 99, 101, 102, 103, 104, 105
McMullan, Jimmy, 55, 66
Mercer, Joe, 31
Mitten, Charlie, 68
Morgans, Kenny, 94
Mozart, WA, 66
Mulligan, Mr, 36
Murphy, Jimmy, 28, 29, 53, 55, 57, 62, 65, 68, 69, 70, 71, 72, 73, 78, 79, 80, 82, 83, 84, 85, 92, 96, 97, 98, 101, 102, 104, 108, 112
Neville, Gary, 1
Neville, Phil, 1
Olive, Les, 54
Palmer, Arnold, 73
Pearce, P, 101
Pearson, Mark, 52
Pegg, David, 33, 46, 47, 53, 91, 97, 101
Pele, -, 16, 91
Powell, Arthur, 81, 82, 101, 105
Presley, Elvis, 57
Puskas, Ferenc, 66
Queenan, ?, 94
Ramsey, Alf, 8
Revie, Don, 29
Richards, Joe, 90
Rhodes, R, 101
Rocca, Louis, 28
Rowe, Arthur, 35
Sadler, David, 22

Savile, Jimmy, 57
Scanlon, Albert, 4, 7, 8, 34, 43, 45, 46, 47, 48, 51, 91, 97, 101, 108
Scholes, Paul, 1
Sebes, Gusztav, 45
Sobers, Garry, 16
Stiles, Nobby, 3, 22, 35, 36
Taylor, Ernie, 83
Taylor, Tommy, 53
Viollet, Dennis, 33, 35, 46, 58, 65, 67, 74
Watson, Mrs, 53
Whalley, Bert, 29, 68, 69, 70, 79, 80, 81, 101, 102
Whelan, Liam (Billy), 33, 47, 65, 91, 97, 101
Whitefoot, Jeff, 46
Winterbottom, Walter, 65
Wright, Billy, 22

QUOTED WRITERS

Clarke, Alf, 18
Csandi, Arpad, 65
Dunning, Eric, 10, 11, 14, 15, 41, 59, 108, 110, 111
Dunphy, Eamon, 19, 20, 44, 53, 54, 55, 57, 66, 68, 79, 84, 92, 102
Elias, Norbert, 10, 11, 13, 14, 15, 41, 59, 108
Fabian, AH, 89
Fishwick, Nicholas, 17, 27
Giddens, Anthony, 10
Glanville, Rick, 19, 54, 66
Green, Geoffrey, 17, 31, 52, 89
Guttman, Allen, 13
Hargreaves12
Hopcraft, Arthur, 17, 22, 32

Hughes, Charles, 65
Huizinga, Johann, 15, 27, 45, 62, 73, 75, 77, 85, 110, 112
Jamrich, Klara, 45
Keller, Hans, 16, 62, 73, 74, 75, 77, 85, 110
Kerrigan, Colm, 26
Kitchin, Lawrence, 11
Lovejoy, Joe, 28
Marie-Brohm, Jean, 13
Marwick, Arthur, 22
Marx, Karl, 12
Mason, Tony, 17, 26, 110
Masterson, DW, 16, 62, 110
McIntosh, Peter, 73
Meek, David, 18
Meisl, Hugo, 18, 76, 77
Michelet, Jules, 4
Miles, Barry, 74
Miller, David, 19, 31, 34, 65, 71
Roberts, John, 18, 54, 58
Taylor, Rogan, 3, 17, 45, 64, 76
Tyrrell, Tom, 18
Wade, Allen, 65
Walvin, James, 17, 110,
Ward, Andrew, 3, 17, 64, 76
Whiting, HTA, 16, 62, 110
Young, Percy, 17, 18, 22, 110

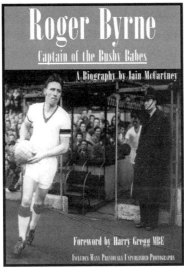

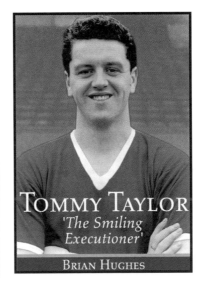

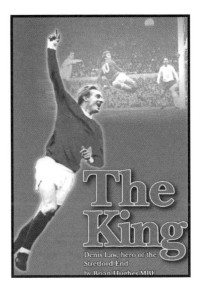

STARMAKER

THE UNTOLD STORY OF
JIMMY MURPHY

BY BRIAN HUGHES MBE

£16.95 - 268 PP - HARDBACK

'My first signing and my most important'

SIR MATT BUSBY

The 'greatest coach in the world' trained the likes of George Best, Duncan Edwards, Bobby Charlton and Dennis Viollet and saved the club in the the wake of the Munich air disaster.

ROGER BYRNE

Captain of the Busby Babes
by Iain McCartney

£16.95 - 189PP - HARDBACK

Despite clashes with authority, Byrne remained fiercely loyal to his manager, team-mates and United's growing army of supporters. By 1958 he and Matt Busby had forged a team of great talent and great resource only for the Munich air disaster to take the Babes away. Who knows how good Roger's team could have become if fate had not intervened?

THE TOMMY TAYLOR STORY

by Brian Hughes

£9.95 - 224PP - PAPERBACK

As the spearhead of the great Busby Babes side, Tommy Taylor was deadly in the air but also able to drift wide and pull defenders out of position. He went onto make 189 appearances for United and won 19 England caps. But it is as a 'big feller with a big heart' that supporters remember 40 years after his death in the Munich air disaster.

VIOLLET

LIFE OF A LEGENDARY GOALSCORER

by Brian Hughes

£10.95 - 334PP - PAPERBACK

A legendary goalscorer and Busby Babe, Dennis Viollet's career took in tragedy and triumph in equal measure. As a player he thrilled thousands as an outstanding teenage footballer with Manchester United's all-conquering Babes. Later, having survived the Munich air disaster, Viollet broke Manchester United's record for goals in a season - a mark he still holds.

THE KING

DENIS LAW, HERO OF THE STRETFORD END

by Brian Hughes MBE

£18.95 - 403PP - HARDBACK

Denis Law was hero and villain all rolled into one: a player capable of incredible feats of skill and power, all carried off with the knowing smile and villainous touch that put some in mind of a Piccadilly pickpocket. To Mancunians, this son of an Aberdonian trawlerman became part of the fabric of the city; first as a dynamic frontman for the Sky Blues and later as an all-action hero at Matt Busby's United.

TO ORDER ANY OF THESE BOOKS CALL 0161 872 3319 OR EMAIL: ENQUIRIES@EMPIRE-UK.COM

COMPLETISTS DELIGHT
The Full Empire Back List

ISBN	Title	Author	Price
1901746003	SF Barnes: His Life and Times	A Searle	£14.95
1901746011	Chasing Glory	R Grillo	£7.95
190174602X	Three Curries and a Shish Kebab	R Bott	£7.99
1901746038	Seasons to Remember	D Kirkley`	£6.95
1901746046	Cups For Cock-Ups+	A Shaw	£8.99
1901746054	Glory Denied	R Grillo	£8.95
1901746062	Standing the Test of Time	B Alley	£16.95
1901746070	The Encyclopaedia of Scottish Cricket	D Potter	£9.99
1901746089	The Silent Cry	J MacPhee	£7.99
1901746097	The Amazing Sports Quiz Book	F Brockett	£6.99
1901746100	I'm Not God, I'm Just a Referee	R Entwistle	£7.99
1901746119	The League Cricket Annual Review 2000	ed. S. Fish	£6.99
1901746143	Roger Byrne - Captain of the Busby Babes	I McCartney	£16.95
1901746151	The IT Manager's Handbook	D Miller	£24.99
190174616X	Blue Tomorrow	M Meehan	£9.99
1901746178	Atkinson for England	G James	£5.99
1901746186	Think Cricket	C Bazalgette	£6.00
1901746194	The League Cricket Annual Review 2001	ed. S. Fish	£7.99
1901746208	Jock McAvoy - Fighting Legend *	B Hughes	£9.95
1901746216	The Tommy Taylor Story*	B Hughes	£8.99
1901746224	Willie Pep*+	B Hughes	£9.95
1901746232	For King & Country*+	B Hughes	£8.95
1901746240	Three In A Row	P Windridge	£7.99
1901746259	Viollet - Life of a legendary goalscorer+PB	R Cavanagh	£16.95
1901746267	Starmaker	B Hughes	£16.95
1901746283	Morrissey's Manchester	P Gatenby	£5.99
1901746305	The IT Manager's Handbook (e-book)	D Miller	£17.99
1901746313	Sir Alex, United & Me	A Pacino	£8.99
1901746321	Bobby Murdoch, Different Class	D Potter	£10.99
190174633X	Goodison Maestros	D Hayes	£5.99
1901746348	Anfield Maestros	D Hayes	£5.99
1901746364	Out of the Void	B Yates	£9.99
1901746356	The King - Denis Law, hero of the...	B Hughes	£17.95
1901746372	The Two Faces of Lee Harvey Oswald	G B Fleming	£8.99
1901746380	My Blue Heaven	D Friend	£10.99
1901746399	Viollet - life of a legendary goalscorer	B Hughes	£11.99
1901746402	Quiz Setting Made Easy	J Dawson	£7.99
1901746437	Catch a Falling Star	N Young	£17.95

* Originally published by Collyhurst & Moston Lads Club
+ Out of print   PB **Superceded by Paperback edition**